Bedtime

Bedtime

INSPIRATIONAL BEDS, BEDROOMS & BOUDOIRS

CELIA FORNER

Foreword by Gianluca Longo

VENDOME

NEW YORK · LONDON

Foreword

Gianluca Longo

Waking up in one of the beautifully decorated rooms at Houghton Hall; looking out over the mesmerizing blue sea up to Capri from one of the balconies at Le Sirenuse in Positano; watching a favorite Netflix series under the duvet; having breakfast served with a kiss ... They all share one very comfortable thing: the bed.

As this book so vividly explores, the bed is a wonderful creation—where life often begins, and ends; where we open our eyes to start the day, and stretch out our legs at the end of it. This is where we play with our parents, when children, and with our partners, when grown-ups, and where we let ourselves get lost in dreams, or nightmares. The bed is also a comfort zone, a kind of limbo, a secure place. In bed we cry, we laugh, we think; we find warmth and reassurance; and, very rarely, we begin quarrels.

Bed is also where our energies are recharged. Research has shown that sleeping on a comfortable bed can boost our mood, and as for how much sleep we need, Napoleon believed the ideal was six hours for a man, seven for a woman, and eight for a fool—worthy of note!

In these pages, Celia Forner captures our intimate relationship with the bed and bedroom, providing style inspiration from different eras, from the ancient to the present day, and documenting significant moments in famous lives, all set in the context of the bedroom. How fascinating that English socialite Stephen Tennant spent the last 17 years of his life in bed at Wilsford, his family manor in Wiltshire, which he had redecorated by Syrie Maugham. John Lennon and Yoko Ono held a press conference from their bed at the Amsterdam Hilton Hotel during their honeymoon in 1969, as part of their "bed-in for peace" protest—one of the most famous events to ever happen in a bed. And who doesn't remember the iconic Cecil Beaton photos of Marylin Monroe in bed?

Passing throug an underground station in London one day, I was caught by an @allontheboard poem that encapsulates the essence of "bed" so wonderfully:

> *I love my bed, my bed loves me;*
>
> *My bed is an island, the floor is the sea,*
>
> *The pillow is a cloud, where I rest my head;*
>
> *The duvet is a mountain that's softer than bread.*
>
> *It's always spring on that island, whatever the weather;*
>
> *We have the same dreams, and share adventures together ...*
>
> *The mattress is the land, a paradise of foam;*
>
> *My bed is an island, that always welcomes me home.*

And yes, the bed is indeed an island: so hard to leave, but so welcoming when we return.

Introduction

Celia Forner

My love story with beds, and bedrooms, began when I was six years old, confined to bed for many months after an accident. It certainly stimulated my imagination as a child, shaping my future self, and perhaps planting the idea for this book. Later, I took comfort in knowing that I was not alone in my experience. Teenage Frida Kahlo was bedridden for months after being paralyzed in a traffic accident, prompting her mother to set up an easel so Frida could paint to alleviate her boredom. John F. Kennedy became a voracious reader during prolonged spells in bed as a sickly child, and Bram Stoker hinted that the seed for Dracula was sown during the author's youth, spent immobile in bed.

Historically, the bed is one of life's most significant locations: where we enter the world, and depart it; where political alliances are formed, kingdoms conquered, love cemented, and where drama unfolds; the site of tragedy, myth, and fable. Our modern predilection for cocooning is a natural extension of this tradition, a reflection of our personal ambitions, fears, tastes, and habits. Each of us has a unique relationship with our bed, as this book so intriguingly explores.

We often get our best ideas in bed. It's where we are at our most vulnerable, and most secure— where we choose to hide from the world. I love to work in mine, reading, writing, or watching movies while taking notes. And I subscribe to the credo of the eccentric English poet Edith Sitwell, who once quipped that "all women should have a day a week in bed." Sitwell shares the company of other writers who found both refuge and inspiration between the sheets, or on top of them. Her namesake Edith Wharton retreated to bed to be free of her corset, and likewise allow her mind to be unrestricted. Truman Capote declared himself a "completely horizontal author," unable to think unless he was lying down with a cigarette and coffee within arm's reach. But William Wordsworth may well have set the bar for bed lazing: while writing poetry under the covers he would simply start from scratch if he lost a sheet of paper over the side, since looking for it was just too much effort.

This book is about extraordinary beds, and the unique bedrooms of exceptional people. Intended to inspire and inform, it entices the reader into beautiful beds throughout history, and across style genres, from classical to post-modern, from minimal to maximal. *Bedtime* has been a joy to work on, and I hope that it proves as satisfying for you as it has been for me.

P2: The grand early 18th-century tester bed in the Wentworth bedroom at Milton Hall, restored with a specially woven silk damask.
P4: Mae West in *Goin' to Town* (1935), directed by Alexander Hall.
P6/7: The Pink Room at Château de Roquetaillade, 1868, in a watercolor on paper by Edmond Duthoit (1837–1889). **LEFT:** A blue set by Marcel Vertès (1895–1961) featured in *Vogue*, May 1953, with photography by Horst P. Horst.

Origins

A Brief History of the Bed Chamber

In 2011, archaeologists in South Africa discovered the world's oldest mattress. Found in a cave, the sleeping mat was 77,000 years old, fashioned from layers of reeds and rushes, and topped with a covering of Cape quince, a medicinal plant known for its ability to repel insects. It shows just how ingenious humans could be in the quest to make bedtime a pleasure.

A century earlier, in 1911, archaeologists at Saqqara, Egypt, were excavating the tomb of Hesy-Ra, scribe to King Djoser, when they came across a set of wall paintings that are thought to depict the world's first bed frames, elevating the sleeper from the cold ground, rodents, and insects. Subsequent excavations uncovered the bed frame belonging to Queen Hetepheres, expertly crafted from wood, covered in gold sheeting, and decorated with a design of feather and flower rosettes.

Dating from around the same period, between 2000 and 1000 BC, terracotta artefacts from Ancient Babylon show erotic scenes of couples in beds like those of the Egyptians. Their bed frames are designed with slots through which a sleeping mat could be attached. Woven or plaited from wool, or wool mixed with goat hair, the mats vary widely in design patterning, with no two the same. It seems that from the start, we wanted our beds to be personalised works. In Ancient Rome, wealthy householders spent lavishly on expensive fabric coverings for their beds, to the extent that one man feigned illness so that friends would visit him in bed and admire his beautiful bed linen, according to the Roman poet Martial.

Our quest for both individuality and comfort at bedtime was uniquely interpreted in China, where Song dynasty citizens rested their heads on ceramic pillows during the hot, humid summers. Shaped into auspicious figures—a lotus, a tiger, a dragon—or embellished with landscapes or sayings from Confucius or Buddha, these pillows were more than functional. They provided inspiration and emotional comfort to the weary. Although the Chinese eventually adopted the raised beds of Europeans, the Japanese retained their habit of sleeping on futon mattresses that were rolled out every evening on tatami matting, and put away the next morning.

Meanwhile, in medieval Europe, even those who could afford to have a separate bedroom kept their beds on display in public living areas. In fact, beds had become major assets, especially four-posters, artistically carved, decorated with jewels, and draped with a canopy and curtains of heavy velvet, not only to keep out drafts, but as a mark of wealth and status. They were handed down from generation to generation, along with feather-and-down mattresses and linen sheets. By the time of the Renaissance, the role of the bed had become cemented in popular and high culture. In religious paintings and portraiture, beds are symbolic of social stature, but also represent the importance of alliances cemented through marriage, between aristocratic and merchant families, and most especially between royal dynasties.

P10: A candlelit grotto in the Italian medieval village of Civitella d'Agliano. **OPPOSITE:** Ancient Greek style reproduced in the 1900s by archaeologist Théodore Reinach and architect Emmanuel Pontremoli at Villa Kérylos, Beaulieu-sur-Mer, France. **ABOVE:** Cubiculum from a villa at Boscoreale, Pompeii, with walls decorated in frescoes dating from c. 50 BC. The bed is inlaid with ivory, paste, and precious stones. **P14:** Cupid reclines on a crimson counterpane in "Venus Admonishing Cupid" (1555–1565), a tapestry designed by Giovanni Battista Castello (1509–1569) based on the story of Cupid and Psyche. **P15, ABOVE:** Krishna in his yellow dhoti converses with a messenger while his feminine counterpart, Radha, beckons from the bedchamber in a watercolor of Krishna and the jester, Basohli, c. 1660–1695. **P15, BELOW:** Two Japanese girls sleep on futons rolled out on tatami matting, their heads resting on ceramic pillows, c. 1880.

ABOVE: A traditional Peranakan bed, possibly built in the 1890s, at Tun Tan Cheng Lock mansion, Singapore. It is typical of the ornate style of a Peranakan wedding bed, with gilded relief work on a red lacquered background, usually on a base of cedarwood. The wedding bed was part of a suite of matching furniture that included a cupboard, washstand, dressing table, and two armchairs with matching footstools. Peranakan culture and architecture evolved from the ethnic Chinese-Malays who began settling along the Malay archipelago from the 10th century onward. OPPOSITE: The bedroom of Kenya-based artist Yony Waite. P18/19: A hidden bed enclosed in a wall of *trompe l'oeil* cabinetry at a Danish farmhouse (c. 1748) in Toftum Village, Denmark. The tradition of the "closet" bed dates to late medieval western Europe. It offered privacy in homes with only one room, and by keeping the sleeping area closed off from the rest of the room, it could be kept warm through body heat.

Kings & Queens

Royal Rooms, Palaces & State Apartments

Centuries before supermodels could claim the right to stay in bed until paid enough to do otherwise, the monarchs of France made lounging in bed not only a privilege but a matter of state. When the king or queen retired to bed, or arose, up to 100 courtiers thronged the royal bedchamber. Attendance at the *lever* (rising ceremony) and *coucher* (bedtime ceremony) was obligatory for the palace inner circle, and the task of dressing or undressing the monarch went not to a servant but to the highest ranking noble.

By the end of the 17th century, the elaborate ritual of the *lever* had evolved into a prolonged spell in bed during which royalty would receive important visitors. This necessitated ornate "parade" beds, so called because this is where you could observe a parade of anyone worth meeting in the realm. Louis XV tired of the constant attention and built a smaller, private bedchamber for himself. His predecessor, however, Louis XIV, apparently relished the attention, and his parade bedroom became the centre of activity at Versailles, not least for female courtiers who competed with one another for a private invitation to the state bed. Marie Antoinette, France's last queen before the French Revolution, adored her beautiful bedroom but was heard to complain, "If only I could spend more time in it alone, with none of my *femmes de chambre* ... it would be perfect."

Toward the end of the 18th century, the idea of the bedroom as a private domain became fashionable. Royalty stopped receiving dignitaries from the comfort of bed, and the bedroom was reserved for intimate activities. The mirrored master bedroom of Jodhpur's Maharaja was nevertheless a busy place, with nine wives and 31 concubines reputedly coming and going. Joséphine Bonaparte also devised her bedrooms as places of seduction, strategically placing mirrors to create the effect of an orgy. At her home in Malmaison she kept two beds: a formal red-and-gilt tented affair, and a simpler one dressed with white cambric and lace-trimmed pillows. It is not clear in which bed she gasped her final breath, but it is well documented that when Napoléon heard the news of her death he went to bed and stayed there for three days. A few years later, in 1821, he retired to his beloved camp bed, installed in the drawing room at Longwood House on the island of St. Helena, and never woke. He had taken precautions though, and had his British minders dress him in his uniform of Field Marshal, complete with boots and spurs.

The British were always attuned to a sense of occasion, and the beds of the nation's stately homes were no exception. The English watercolorist William Turner painted several bedrooms at Petworth House, the home of art collector and bohemian Lord Egremont. Turner himself was a frequent guest and seemed to have been in lively company, given the number of paintings of bedrooms with crumpled sheets and pillows. However, the star feature of this stately home was the red damask Petworth State Bed, made for the visit of Charles VI, Holy Roman Emperor and King of Spain, in 1703. Two decades later, a splendid bed upholstered in crimson satin damask was made for George II; he spent his final hours in the bed, which was later given to the 4th Duke of Devonshire at Chatsworth House. Death, birth, and sex in the royal bed, often witnessed by court officials, were of enormous significance, deciding the future of the monarchy and the prospects of the nation.

P20: In the Paço Ducal, the luxurious palace of the Dukes of Braganza in Vila Viçosa, the royal cradle is nestled in an alcove draped with baby-blue curtains. A gilded cherub holds a lace canopy above the crib. P22/23: The imposing state bedroom suite of Empress Alexandra Feodorovna, a granddaughter of Queen Victoria, at the Anichkov Palace, St. Petersburg, Russia. Watercolor by Eduard Petrovich Hau (1807–1887).

ABOVE: Built from oak around 1700 and upholstered in Chinese silk, the Melville Bed was commissioned by the 1st Earl of Melville for his home in Fife, Scotland. It was probably designed by Daniel Marot (1661–1752). OPPOSITE: The State Bed at Petworth House in England, made in the 1750s, is considered a rococo masterpiece. Pamela Wyndham, Lady Egremont, slept here after her husband inherited the house in the 1950s, her pet owl apparently nesting overhead in the gilt branches.

OPPOSITE: The bedroom of King Ferdinand II in the Palácio de Pena in Sintra, Portugal, a former Hieronymite monastery, which the king transformed into a royal home between 1840 and 1845. It is considered the ultimate expression of 19th-century Portuguese Romanticism. A great supporter of the arts, Ferdinand II had the bedroom suite decorated with panache. The walls and vaulted ceiling are covered in ornate Moorish-style tiles made by ceramicist Wenceslau Cifka, a personal friend of Ferdinand II.

ABOVE: On the 1st floor of medieval Powis Castle in Wales is a state bedroom that has survived since the 1660s without remodeling, although the bed itself is from around 1760. It is made from mahogany, oak, and giltwood, and is upholstered with red cut-velvet hangings from Spitalfields in London, which at the time was renowned for the skill of its textile makers. This type of canopied bed is also known as a "tester."

LEFT: The bedroom of Empress Joséphine at Château de Malmaison, the home she shared with Napoléon just west of Paris. The room was decorated around 1805 by designer Louis-Martin Berthault, who draped the entire room with fabric to create the impression of a tent, referencing Napoléon's military campaigns. **ABOVE:** Napoléon Bonaparte's canopied bed, made from mahogany and gilded bronze, in his quarters at Château de Malmaison. The classical Roman motifs are typical of Empire style. **P30, TOP LEFT:** A bedroom at Hermesvilla, a palace in the Lainzer Tiergarten in Vienna, a former hunting ground for the Habsburg nobility. Emperor Franz Joseph I gave the property to his wife Empress Elisabeth. **P30, BELOW LEFT:** At his winter palace in Vienna, Eugene, Prince of Savoy, slept in a baroque bed adorned with militaristic imagery, including Ottomans and Imperial warriors. **P31:** Frescoes depicting "The Rape of the Sabines," attributed to Sir James Thornhill, cover the walls of the "Sabine Room" at historic Chatsworth House, Derbyshire, England.

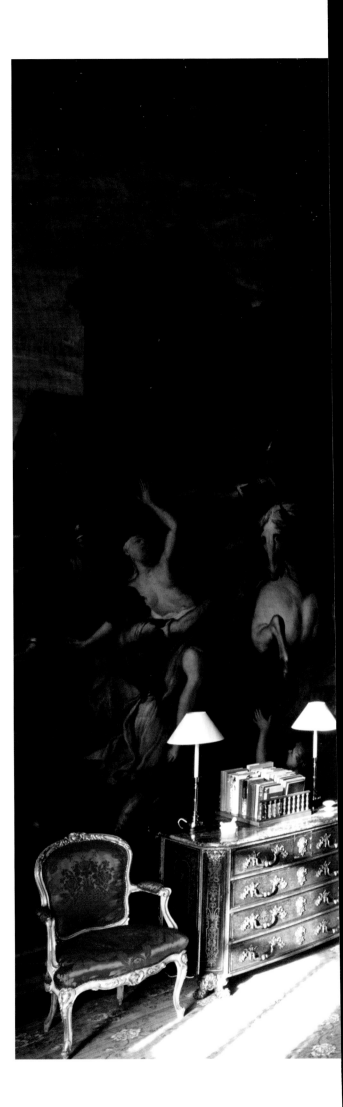

LEFT: Empress Josephine never saw the bedroom built for by Napoléon at the 18th-century Chateau de Compiègne, decorated in 1808-09 in the First French Empire style. By the time it was finished, Napoléon had remarried and so his second wife, Empress Marie-Louise moved in. The tapissier Darrac provided the rich textiles for the bed, which is by François-Honoré-Georges Jacob-Desmalter (1770-1841), as is the other furniture in the room. The painted wall decoration is by Dubois & Redoute. The paintings are by Anne-Louis Girodet (1767-1824). **ABOVE:** The King of Rome's bedroom at the Chateau de Compiègne. The bed was made in 1808 by Pierre-Benoit Marcion (1769-1840).

ABOVE: At Stonor Park, the seat of the Stonor family in Oxfordshire for over 850 years, the Shell Room was originally the bedroom of Sir Francis Stonor, Sheriff of Oxfordshire. It is named for its centerpiece, a Napoleonic bed in the style of a shell, supported by gilt mermaids and dolphins and complemented by oyster-shaped chairs. **OPPOSITE:** A bedroom at the Palazzo Davanzati, built in Florence in the mid 14th century. It is an unusual example of the transitional style between medieval and Renaissance.

OPPOSITE: The Duke of Genoa's bedroom is a baroque fantasy, housed in the Palazzo Reale, Genoa. Built in the 17th century, the palace was expanded and remodeled in the 18th century with the additon of baroque elements. It became a UNESCO World Heritage site in 2006. ABOVE: The State Bedroom at Pavlovsk Palace, St. Petersburg. Behind the giltwood armchairs by Henri Jacob is a tempera painting on silk of "The Attributes of Spring" by Johann Jacob Mettenleiter from a sketch by Willem van Leen.

ABOVE: *A Room to Sleep In* (1885) by the artist Durin, which featured in *The Eighteenth Century: Its Institutions, Customs and Costumes: France 1700-1789*, by Paul Lacroix. **RIGHT:** Bedroom from the Sagredo Palace in Venice, with stuccowork attributed to Abbondio Stazio. **OPPOSITE:** One of the bedrooms reserved for ambassadors who stayed at the Castello di Masino, near Turin, the family seat of the counts of Valperga. The ceiling is decorated with the coats of arms of European dynasties connected with the Valpargas. The room features fine examples of *pastiglia di riso* (rice powder stucco) and has an unusual 19th-century writing desk. **P40:** The Embroidered Bedchamber at Houghton Hall, Norfolk, England. **P41:** Queen Marie Antoinette's State Bedroom at the Palace of Versailles dates from 1787, with restored summer decoration.

P42/43: A restored bedroom at the medieval Château de Roquetaillade, with half-tester bed and mantelpiece adorned with a woman's head. The original decoration was conceived by Eugene Viollet-le-Duc. **OPPOSITE:** The Wellington Bedroom at historic Chatsworth House, Derbyshire, England. **ABOVE:** The Green Velvet Bedchamber at Houghton Hall, Norfolk, England, built between 1722 and 1735 for Sir Robert Walpole, the first prime minister of Great Britain. It features the famous Shell bed designed by William Kent c. 1732. Made from oak and pine, the frame is hung with green silk velvet adorned with silver gilt embroidery and fringing. The shell of Venus on the headboard is echoed in the ceiling, tapestries, and fireplace design.

P46, TOP LEFT: The bedroom of Elizabeth of Bavaria, Schloss Tegernsee c. 1840, watercolor on paper by Franz Xavier Nachtmann (1799–1846). P46, BELOW LEFT: A pair of enormous stoves, made around 1740 by the ceramicist Gottfried Kater, flank an alcove housing a half-tester bed in the Duke's Bedroom at the Rundale Palace, Latvia. This state bedroom is located in the center of the palace, in keeping with the tradition of Versailles. P47: The Wellington Room at Chatsworth House is named after the Duke who slept here in 1843. The walls are covered in Chinese wallpaper from the 1830s, and the *lit à la Polonaise* is hung with green damask curtains. OPPOSITE: A Florentine mahogany bed in the Empire style, with chiseled bronze sculptures. The design is Italian and dates from 1820. ABOVE: A tartan-covered sleigh bed is draped in green and cream silk in this contemporary London dressing room, which reprises the popular fashion for tented interiors and camp furniture during the Napoleonic era.

ABOVE: Emperor Napoléon's camp bed, hat, and binoculars, at the Musée de l'Armée, Paris. RIGHT: The tented room in the Charlottenhof Palace, Potsdam, decorated around 1830, as depicted in a watercolor by Karl Friedrich Schinkel (1781–1841), the architect who built the neoclassical palace. Fashioned in the style of a Roman emperor's tent, the guest room's blue and white striped wallcoverings and ceiling are matched by the canopied beds and window treatments. The blue and white scheme echoed the heraldic colors of Bavaria, the birthplace of Elisabeth, wife of King Frederick William IV of Prussia, whose summer residence was Charlottenhof. Explorer Alexander von Humboldt often stayed in this room during the summers of 1835–1840.

ABOVE: The drawing room at Stanway House, a Jacobean manor in Gloucestershire, England, is dominated by a pair of 18th-century Chinese daybeds made by Thomas Chippendale. The renowned cabinet maker was famed for his chinoserie furniture. OPPOSITE: An 18th-century chinoiserie bedroom at Badminton House in Gloucestershire, with hand-painted wallpaper and furniture by William and John Linnell. Inspired by Chinese pagodas, the bed was made in London by the Linnells around 1754 from beechwood, japanned in red, yellow, and blue, and gilded. P54/55: The bedroom of Lady Fitzwilliam at Milton Hall in Cambridgeshire, England, is lined with hand-painted mid-18th-century Chinese wallpaper in fretwork-patterned borders. The house has been the family seat of the Fitzwilliam family since 1594.

OPPOSITE: Bought at auction 40 years ago, this 18th-century bed, which now stands in the "Best Guest Bedroom" at Upton Wold in Gloucestershire, England, was badly damaged by fire and took 15 months to restore. **ABOVE:** The four-poster bed in Mary, Queen of Scots, bedroom at Hardwick Hall, Derbyshire, England, is upholstered in black velvet embroidered with gold thread. Although there is no evidence that Mary, Queen of Scots, ever stayed at Hardwick Hall, a myth persisted that she spent some of her imprisonment at the house. The bed itself is made of English oak, with a headboard of red damask overlaid with red silk. The black velvet is thought to be 19th century, appliquéd with embroidery from the late 16th or early 17th century.

OPPOSITE: The master of Art Deco furniture design, Émile-Jacques Ruhlmann (1879–1933), created this suite in the Art Deco palace of Morbi, built between 1931 and 1944 in the Indian state of Gujarat. The mural behind the bed is by Stefan Norblin. Mosquito-net curtains hang from a recessed curtain track in the ceiling relief. ABOVE: A bedroom in the Dholpur Raj Niwas Palace, Rajasthan, India, where the architect chose to cover the walls with tiles in fresh blue and green tones, providing visual relief from the sweltering summers of the region. LEFT: The Umaid Bhawan Palace, home of the Maharaja of Jodhpur, is the last of the great Indian palaces, decorated in Art Deco style. P60/61: This bedroom at the Royal Oasis, an annex to the Wankaner Palace in Gujarat, India, where members of the royal family spent their summers, was inspired by the European Art Deco style. P62: The Cabinet Room at Houghton Hall, Norfolk, England, was originally used by owner Sir Robert Walpole to display part of his extensive art collection, but later became a bedroom. The walls were covered with silvered, hand-painted chinoiserie paper, and hung with rococo mirrors. P63: The Queen's Bedchamber for the first wife of Louis XIV, Maria Theresa of Spain, in Château de Chambord, the largest of the Loire Valley castles.

P64: An 18th-century bed in the house of Prince Vincenzo Caracciolo d'Aquara in Naples. P65: Medieval Issogne Castle, seat of the Bishops of Aosta in Italy, was transformed into a luxurious home by George of Challant from 1490 to 1509. This bedroom typifies the castle decor with its intricate coffered ceilings and colorful frescoed walls. ABOVE: Dutch tiles decorate the walls of the sleeping quarters in the Maharaja's palace inside Jaisalmer Fort, Rajasthan, India. OPPOSITE: The walls and ceiling of this twin bedroom in an Indian palace are lined with metallic tiles. P68/69: The Art Deco bedroom of Virginia Courtauld at Eltham Palace in London has curved walls lined with maple flexwood. The home of textile magnates Stephen and Virginia Courtauld in the 1930s, Eltham was decorated by Peter Malacrida, an Italian aristocrat and fashionable interior designer of the day. For Virginia's bedroom, Malacrida concealed the main heating and lighting sources in the ceiling, which allowed the room to remain uncluttered.

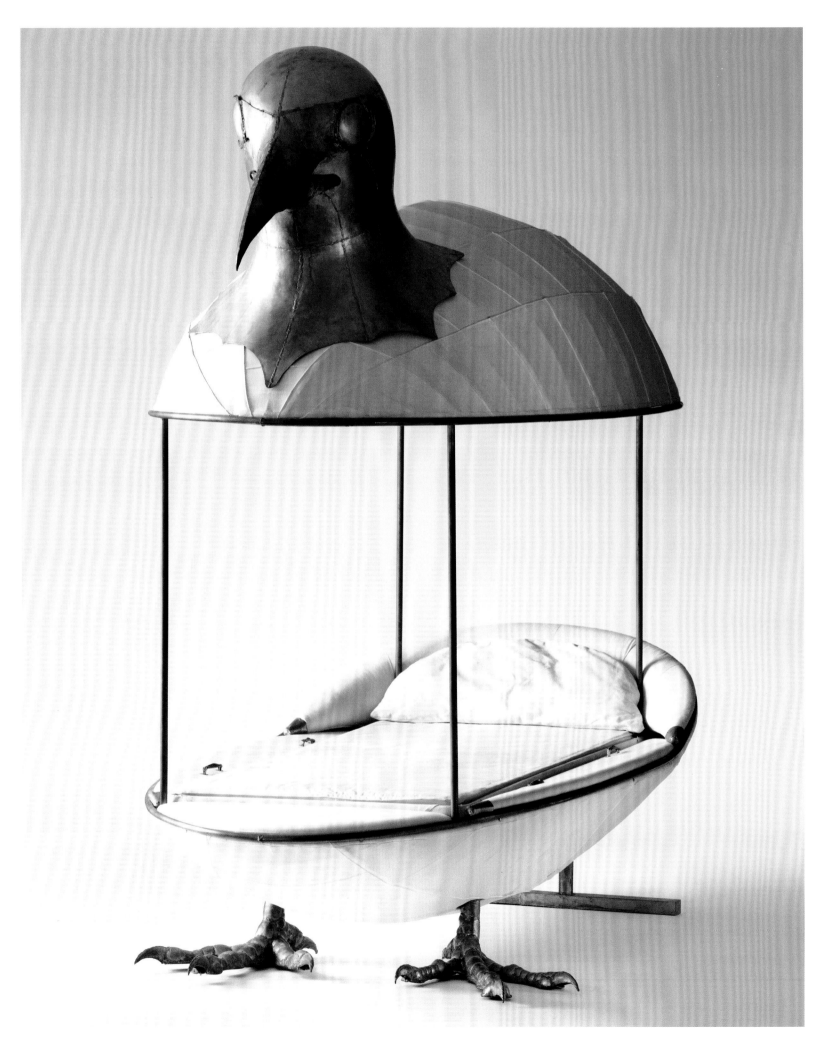

Sleeping by Design

Designers & Decorators, At Home & At Work

Mademoiselle Choupette, the celebrity cat of the late Karl Lagerfeld, declared in an online interview that she never suffered from jetlag since she always slept well, surrounded by fine sheets and plump pillows. "Doesn't everyone have a bedroom on the plane?" she purred. Her attachment to the notion of a beautiful sleeping space has also been an obsession for many of the great interior designers and architects who have elevated the bed from ordinary to extraordinary.

The rise of the interior decorator in the 20th century proved that in the hands of a creative virtuoso the bed could be far from average, from the exquisite custom furniture of Maison Jansen to the surreal canopied birds of Les Lalanne. One of the first designers to prioritize bedroom design was Charles Rennie Mackintosh, who in the early 1900s created the archetype of the spacious, minimal bedroom, fitted with integrated furniture and flooded with natural light, a theme developed further by celebrated British decorator Syrie Maugham. Meanwhile, Irish architect and interior designer Eileen Gray fully embraced modernism, turning the daybed of the ancient Romans into an industrial-inspired classic.

Early American pioneers of the interior-designed bedroom were anti-minimalists. Sister Parish and her cousin Dorothy Draper forged a lavish style from the 1930s onward that would become known as Modern Baroque or Hollywood Regency. In Europe, postwar bedroom style became more romantic, and the cocooning safety of the bed took on new significance. Jean Royère, for example, fused organic lines, precious materials, and a poetic sensibility into his gilded and canopied "Starlet" bed.

Architect Lorenzo Mongiardino was also a dreamer, using faux finishes and magical effects to create enchanted boudoirs. He was an inspiration for American decorator Tony Duquette—a maximalist, whose bedrooms were the ultimate expression of his style. No less extreme than Duquette in his fantastical approach to the bed, design vigilantes Archizoom positioned themselves as anti-historical. They went out of their way to challenge the idea of what middle classes deemed good taste. With their "Dream Bed" series of 1967, the Italian studio created beds that were as perversely kitsch as they were avant-garde, subverting any logical link to the traditional bedroom. Designing during the same period, Hungarian architect Antti Lovag was also a Futurist, but his bed settings for Pierre Cardin were overtly optimistic, with blazing pop colors and bubble forms.

The modernists evolved a minimalist vision of how we should spend our resting hours, with bedrooms stripped of distractions. Mid-century modernist Albert Frey was influential with his Palm Springs house, in which the bedroom extended into the surrounding desert, the only furnishing the bed itself. Likewise, Philip Johnson's master suite for the Brick House resembled a religious sanctuary, foretelling how, in the next century, the bedroom would become a shrine to sleep.

P70: *Cocodoll*, the "Bird Bed," designed by François-Xavier and Claude Lalanne, 1964. **LEFT:** This original Chippendale chinoiserie four-poster, with its pagoda-style canopy, is topped with a carved figure in a boat. Thomas Chippendale's Chinese-style furniture was the height of fashion for bedrooms in mid-18th-century England, inspiring many copies. The bed shown here was originally made for the family of Lady Randolph Churchill, and much later became part of the collection of New York decorator Harrison Cultra. After his death, clients and friends the Barclays purchased the bed from the Cultra estate as a gift for Hutton Wilkinson, who designed this room to complement the bed. The walls are painted Imperial yellow and hung with panels from antique Coromandel screens in red lacquered frames. **ABOVE:** Reflected in a gilt-framed teardrop, an Empire-style bed in a room designed by David Mlinaric.

ABOVE: Charles Rennie Mackintosh (1868–1928) collaborated with his wife Margaret Macdonald (1864–1933) in 1904 on the ground-breaking interiors of Hill House, in Helensburgh, just outside Glasgow, Scotland, for publisher Walter Blackie. Mackintosh and Macdonald became renowned for their light-filled interiors, the antithesis of the prevailing Victorian Gothic fashion for heavy, dark furnishings. For the master suite at Hill House, known as "The White Bedroom", the couple created an integrated suite in pale tones, merging rectilinear details with feminine forms, including Mackintosh's signature roses, in the Art Nouveau style. **OPPOSITE:** The guest room at 78 Derngate, Northampton, remodeled by Charles Rennie Mackintosh in 1916. This was Mackintosh's last major commission, and the guest room is considered one of his most striking interiors, with black, blue, and white stripes running up the walls and across the ceiling. Mackintosh showed that geometrical rigor had a place in the bedroom, pre-empting modernist principles.

ABOVE: A bedroom designed by Kindel Furniture in homage to American decorator Dorothy Draper (1889–1969). The Michigan furniture firm of Kindel collaborated with Dorothy Draper & Company's Carleton Varney to produce the bedroom suite, inspired by Draper's own bed in her apartment at the Carlyle Hotel in New York. The striped walls and cabbage-rose chintz are typical of the maximalist style that made her one of the leading American interior designers from the 1930s through 1960s. **OPPOSITE:** In the bedroom she designed for the Connecticut summer home of Mr. and Mrs. Henry R. Luce, Draper used her signature cabbage-rose chintz to bring charm to a modern baroque backdrop. A painting by Matisse is hung on the left wall. **P78, ABOVE:** As featured in *Vogue* in 1937, the Paris home of Helena Rubinstein, with bedroom designed by Jansen. **P78, BELOW LEFT:** Designed in 1935 by Harold Chalton Bradshaw (1893–1943) with furniture by Betty Joel (1896–1985), this bedroom exemplified British modernism. **P78, BELOW RIGHT:** A Surrealist bed by artist Carlo Bugatti (1856–1940). **P79:** A suspended bed constructed by Pierre Chareau (1883–1950) on the terrace of poet Comtesse de Noaille's villa in Hygères, France, designed by architect Robert Mallet-Stevens. The steel tube chair is by Marcel Breuer, 1929.

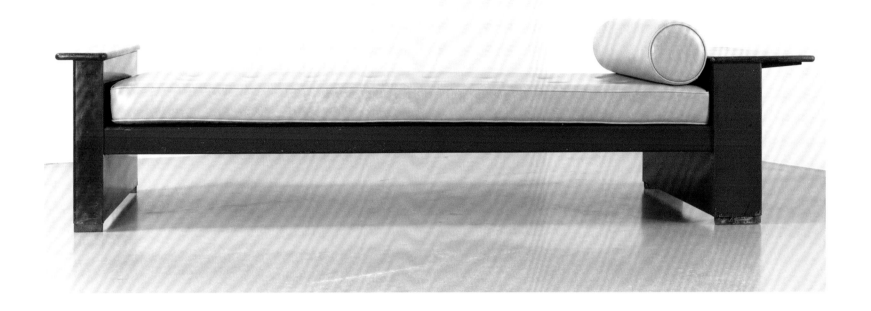

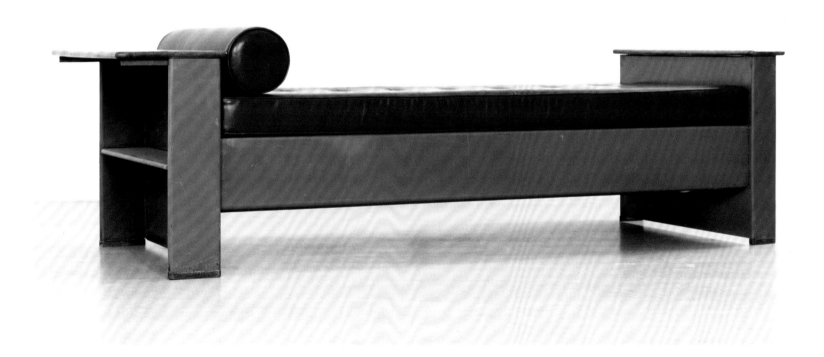

ABOVE: One of 70 beds produced by Jean Prouvé (1901–1984) in 1932 as part of a commission to design the student dormitory interiors for the Cité Universitaire Monbois in Nancy, France. The bed was made of bent sheet steel, enameled in red, and incorporated wooden shelving. It was intended to be robust, easy to clean, and relatively inexpensive to produce. This was among the first public commissions of furniture undertaken using mass-production techniques.

BELOW: Bed No. 102 was produced in a small-scale run of 36 units by Jean Prouvé's atelier in 1936 for the Lycée Fabert boarding school in Metz, France. This model was made from bent steel and oak, and upholstered in leather. The same year Prouvé's workshop had purchased a Pels metal pressing and folding machine, enabling the designer to continue pioneering mass-produced furniture for public projects.

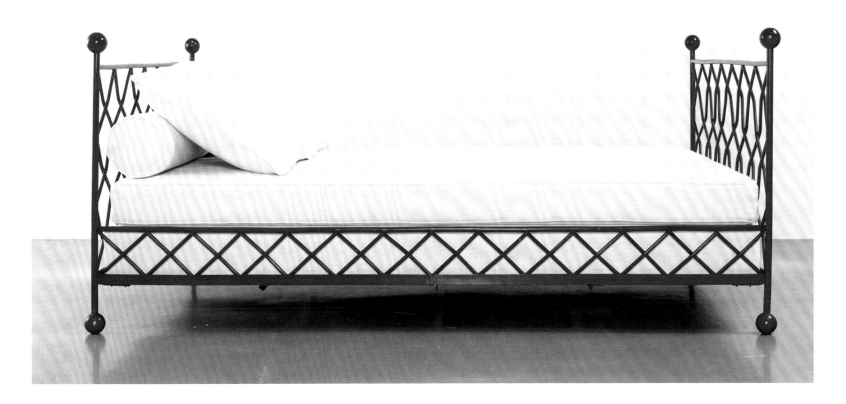

ABOVE: Dating from 1937, a bed designed by André Arbus (1903–1969) is inset with an ivory motif by sculptor Vadim Androusov (1875–1975). At the time, Arbus had recently opened a gallery on Avenue Matignon in Paris, and was on his way to becoming one of the city's most creative furniture makers. This bed was one of a pair of lits bateaux donated to the Musée des Arts Décoratifs, Paris, by Karl Lagerfeld in 1997. BELOW: The *croisillon*, or lattice, motif was a recurring theme in the work of self-taught designer Jean Royère (1902–1981), and gave its name to a wide range of his furniture, including this bed in red-lacquered metal tubing from around 1947. The same year he exhibited a similar-style bed at the Salon des Artistes Décorateurs, and opened a gallery in St. Tropez, as well as an agency in Beirut to capitalize on his growing following in the Middle East. The bed is typical of his fanciful approach and his penchant for combining luxurious and industrial elements.

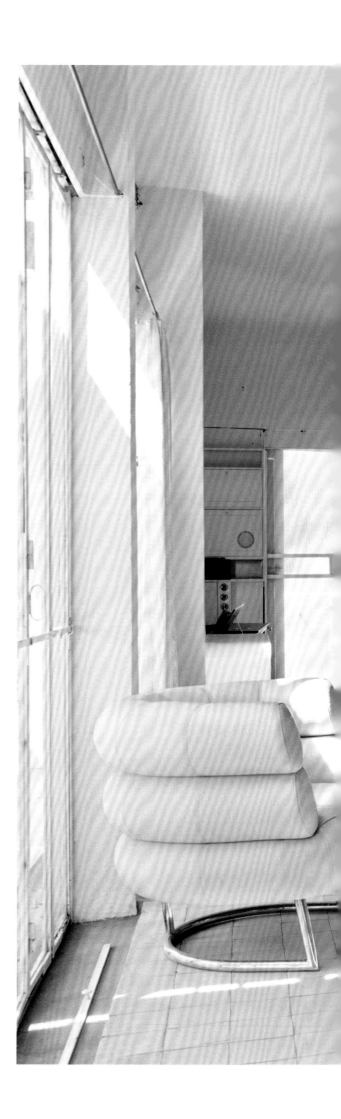

ABOVE: Eileen Gray (1878–1976) staged her first major public showing at the Salon des Artistes Décorateurs, Paris, in 1923 with this
interior exhibit entitled "Room-Boudoir de Monte Carlo." It featured
a divan of zebra wood, a carpet with an abstract design in shades
of blue, brown and gray, and Gray's hand-lacquered Brick Screen,
which was to become a collector's piece. Her vision of how a modern
bedroom could look was the target of criticism from the French
media, but attracted the attention of Bauhaus architect Walter
Gropius and the De Stijl group in The Netherlands. BELOW & RIGHT:
A bedroom at E-1027, the modernist villa at Roquebrune-Cap-
Martin, France, built by Eileen Gray in 1929, before restoration
[above] and after [right]. During restoration, the mural installed by
Le Corbusier (1887–1965) during his tenancy was removed, return-
ing the villa to Gray's original scheme.

OPPOSITE, ABOVE: A canopied bed by Jean Royère, 1947, features the *croisillon*, or lattice pattern, for which he became known. The device is repeated in the suite of furniture for the rest of the room, including the dressing table and chair. OPPOSITE, BELOW LEFT: A Paris bedroom by Jean Royère in 1951. OPPOSITE, BELOW RIGHT: A *trèfle* (clover leaf) bed in painted straw marquetry with star decoration by Jean Royère, dating from 1954.

ABOVE: In a drawing of graphite and gouache from 1935-1937, André Arbus displays the elegant style for which he became renowned. Learning his trade in his father's furniture workshop, Arbus developed a mastery of fine wood veneers, lacquer, vellum and parchment that made his furniture exceptionally sought-after. He combined modernist lines with a neoclassical sensibility.

OPPOSITE: One of two beds realized by Émile-Jacques Ruhlmann (1879–1933) in a design called *Lit Soleil*, so called for the bed-head's resemblance to the sun, with the effect of radiating rays in the woodwork. The bed pictured here was produced in 1923 for Pierre Laurent, Ruhlmann's business partner in Ruhlmann and Laurent. The second bed was made around 1930 for French actress Jane Renouardt. ABOVE: Interior schemes for four bedrooms by

Émile-Jacques Ruhlmann. Top left, right, and below left come from an album of interior drawings entitled *Intimacy No. 4*. Below right is a pochoir stencil of a bedroom for two girls from *Repertoire du Gout Moderne* (Repertoire of Modern Taste), a five-volume compendium published by Albert Levy in Paris in the late 1920s. His aim was to "provide logical, practical, creative solutions to the problems raised by the organization, furnishing, and decoration of an apartment."

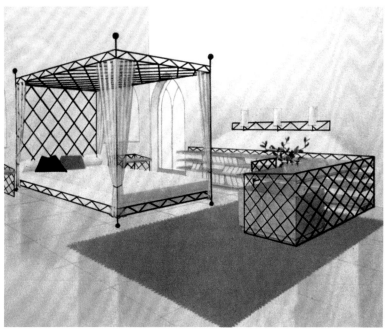

OPPOSITE, ABOVE: A decade before collaborating on the modernist landmark Maison de Verre in Paris, architect Pierre Chareau undertook this bedroom project in 1920. The artwork is by Raoul Dufy (1877-1953). Although he had studied architecture, Chareau initially worked on interior projects and became a leading figure in the decorative arts movement in France. OPPOSITE, BELOW LEFT: Bedroom illustration from the June 1950 issue of *Art et Décoration*. OPPOSITE, BELOW RIGHT: Project for a lady's bedroom, 1925, by André Groult (1884-1966) from *Arts de la Maison*, Bibliothèque des Arts Décoratifs. Groult bridged Art Nouveau and Art Deco styles, producing modern streamlined furniture with gently curved silhouettes. ABOVE: The spare but luxurious style of French designer André Arbus is evident in this bedroom interior scheme from 1937, illustrated in gouache and pencil on paper. His furniture was known for its light, elegant form, and angular details.

LEFT: A Jean Royère bed in a bedroom set conceived by Paris-based architect and interior designer India Mahdavi for Galerie Patrick Seguin at Design Miami 2010. The bed and small table feature Royère's signature lattice pattern in gilded steel. **ABOVE:** Bed with integrated cupboard by Jacques Adnet (1900–1984), made of wood and black lacquer and upholstered with shagren. Adnet was an icon of French modernism, known for the clean lines and unadorned nature of his furniture, as well as his expert use of leather. He was also an innovator, often integrating storage drawers and shelves into his designs. **BELOW:** A bed from 1937 by the avant-garde Art Deco designer Jean-Charles Moreux (1889–1956). He was heavily influenced by Surrealism, and here plays on the theme of the "monster under the bed" with details such as the oversized clawed feet and paw-like bedhead.

ABOVE: A bedroom designed by Marc du Plantier (1901–1975) in the Parisian apartment he shared with his wife Anne on the rue Belvédère in Boulogne-Billancourt, pictured here around 1966.
BELOW: A sketch in crayon and biro on paper of a bedroom suite by Marc du Plantier, dated to 1957. Decorated in shades of violet, forest green and gold, the room featured an upholstered bed against a backdrop of library shelving.

OPPOSITE: The so-called Map Room at Monkton House, part of the West Dean estate in Sussex, designed in 1902 by Sir Edwin Lutyens for Mr. and Mrs. Willie James. The house was inherited by their only son, the poet Edward James, in the 1930s. A passionate supporter of Surrealism, James employed Salvador Dali (1904–1989) as consultant to oversee additions to the house and redecorate it with the help of Kit Nicholson, Sir Hugh Casson, Syrie Maugham, and Norris Wakefield.

OPPOSITE: Design for a bedroom in Tehran, from the late 1950s, by Jean Royère, rendered on paper with pencil and gouache. The room includes two variants of the designer's *Lit Starlet* made from gilded iron tubing. Royère opened an office in Tehran in 1958 after he was approached by the Shah of Iran to design a study and cinema for the Sa'ad Abad Palace. Other commissions followed for the Shah's sisters and daughter. **ABOVE:** A Starlet daybed in metal with gilt patina, c. 1956, by Jean Royère, at an exhibition of his work at the Sonnabend Gallery in 2008, with background setting by India Mahdavi. **P96, ABOVE:** Variant of the egg bed, in oak and mohair velvet, 1959, by Jean Royère, with Liane floor lamp, Eiffel Tower console and table lamp by Max Ingrand. **P96, BELOW:** Bedroom of performer and musician Henri Salvador, with furniture designed by Jean Royère; captured in a watercolor by Anatoly Stolnikoff, France, 1994. **P97:** Design for a bedroom in Athens by Jean Royère, rendered in pencil and gouache on paper.

ABOVE: Architect Philip Johnson (1906–2005) in the bedroom of the Brick House, designed to complement the neighboring Glass House, New Canaan, Conneticut, which he also designed. Both buildings were built between 1945 and 1948, and were Johnson's residence from 1949 until his death in 2005. The Brick House was originally planned as guest quarters, though Johnson eventually slept there. BELOW: The bedroom of the Glass House, designed by Johnson to blend seamlessly with the landscape. Although there are no interior walls, a partition separates the sleeping area from the other living areas; the partition also serves as a headboard for the bed. OPPOSITE: The bedroom of the Brick House was inspired by Filippo Brunelleschi's 15th-century Duomo in Florence. The walls are lined with fabric and the lighting is installed above the free-form ceiling canopy.

ABOVE: The wood- and stone-lined bedroom of the Miller House in Ontario, Canada, designed in 1950 by architect Eero Saarinen (1910–1961) for industrialist J. Irwin Miller as a summer home. The interior spaces were designed by Alexander Girard, using natural materials to reflect the woodland setting, with playful splashes of bright color. **OPPOSITE, ABOVE:** Built from redwood and red brick, Frank Lloyd Wright's (1867–1959) Weltzheimer-Johnson house for Charles and Margaret Weltzheimer incorporated a wing with four

bedrooms. The house was commissioned in 1947 and built between 1948 and 1949 in Oberlin, Ohio. **OPPOSITE BELOW, LEFT:** A bedroom in the Jacobs House II, Middleton Wisconsin, designed by Frank Lloyd Wright and built between 1946 and 1948. It was the second house commissioned by Herbert and Katherine Jacobs. **OPPOSITE BELOW, RIGHT:** The living area at the Villa Sarabhai, built by architect Le Corbusier in Ahmedabad, India, 1951–55, is furnished with a rustic Indian daybed against a wall of cedarwood.

ABOVE: The winter bedroom in designer Madeleine Castaing's (1894–1992) former home, Maison de Lèves, near Chartres, France. An antique, swan-necked iron bed with a quilted base is canopied with white, tasseled muslin, creating a romantic vignette typical of the designer, who was known for her pairing of rare furnishings and humble materials. The carpet was made to her own design. Referring to her romantic, and often unexpected, interior combinations, Castaing once said, "I decorate houses the way that others paint pictures or write books." **OPPOSITE:** The master bedroom at the Château de Vauboyen, near Paris, was decorated in homage to Madeleine Castaing, using the designer's carpet, fabrics, and furniture. The combination of foliage-themed flooring, muslin curtains edged with delicate pompoms, Empire-style furniture, and sky blue walls is classic Castaing.

ABOVE: One of the guest rooms at the Château de Groussay, in Montfort-l'Amaury, west of Paris, one of many homes belonging to art collector and interior decorator Charles de Beistegui and his family. A patron of the Surrealists and modernists in the 1930s, de Beistegui later embraced historical decoration, collecting important examples of antique French furniture. De Beistegui purchased Château de Groussay in 1939 and spent the next 30 years transforming its interiors.

ABOVE: A guest bedroom in the Maine home of interior designer Sister Parish (1910–1994) (aka Mrs Henry Parish II), credited with developing the American Country look, a homespun take on English Country House style. This guest room is an example of her aesthetic, with its mix of fine furnishings and frugal elements such as the carpet patched together from rug samples. Set between the floral chintz curtains and canopied bed, a painted screen gives the impression of a bird cage.

ABOVE: A reconstruction of the 1940 bedroom of architect Giorgio Devalle's Turin apartment designed by his friend Carlo Mollino (1905-1973), at the Galleria d'Arte Moderna Torino in 2006. Quilted walls in antique rose, a velvet lip-shaped sofa, and opulent curtains evoke Mollino's surreal, erotic interiors. **OPPOSITE, ABOVE:** A bedroom suite designed in 1950 by Hungarian-born American architect and interior designer Paul Laszlo (1900–1993). Known for his bold use of color, Laszlo established a studio on Rodeo Drive in Beverly Hills, Los Angeles, in 1941, and also designed some of Herman Miller's key furniture lines from 1948 to 1952. **OPPOSITE, BELOW:** Designed in 1954–56 by architect Albert Frey (1903–1998), this Palm Springs bedroom reflects the architect's desire to unify nature and humanity. **P108/109:** Frey's Palm Springs House II, completed in 1964, with its bedroom overlooking the desert landscape.

OPPOSITE: In 1944, Jean Prouvé was commissioned to design a prefabricated "Demountable House" for homeless war victims in Lorraine, France. The 6 x 6 meter (approx. 20 x20 foot) open-plan structure could be assembled on site in a day by two people. Although the project was never realized, a few examples remain. This one is furnished with a variant of Prouvé's bed SCAL No. 458 from 1957, with an integrated swivel bedside table by Charlotte Perriand. The painting "Untitled" is by Jean-Michel Basquiat, 1981. **ABOVE:** Bedroom at the home of Robert Silverstein in Beverly Hills, designed in 1961 by architects Jack Charney (1921–) and Sanford Kent (1918-1997). Silverstein's business involved repackaging Japanese toys for the American market, and his Japanese connections are evident in the bedroom design with its low-set bed, floor-level seating, and sliding shoji doors leading out to a rock garden. **BELOW:** A bedroom set showcasing the designs of the Widdicomb Furniture Company, founded in Michigan in 1858. In the 1950s, the company produced bedroom suite collections inspired by Scandinavian, Japanese, and Shaker furniture.

ABOVE: American architect John Lautner (1911–1994) applied organic design principles to this bedroom in the Segel House, in Malibu, USA, completed in 1980. Considered one of his most outstanding projects, the house features curved glass walls and sculptural applications of concrete and wood, including a concrete fireplace in the master bedroom. **BELOW:** One of five bedrooms in Lautner's Stevens House, Malibu, completed in 1969. With interiors of concrete and cedar, the main living areas have sliding glass doors, which open onto views of the beach and allow sea breezes to circulate and cool the rooms. **OPPOSITE:** The master bedroom in the modernist Beverly Hills house of James Goldstein, designed by Lautner and built between 1961 and 1963. A triangular cantilevered deck with swimming pool lies above the master bedroom. The pool itself is held back by a brick wall in the bedroom, inset with viewing windows into the pool.

LEFT: The master bedroom of the Goldstein residence at night, commanding expansive views over Los Angeles through its glass walls. This triangular daybed, with integrated glass side tables, sits beyond the master bed and is set into the nose of the triangular room. After James Goldstein bought the property in 1972, he engaged John Lautner to remodel the house, replacing the original windows, which had been separated by steel mullions, with large sheets of uninterrupted glass.

OPPOSITE: In 1965, David Hicks (1929–1998) transformed Peter and Didi Saunders' bedroom at Easton Grey House, Wiltshire, England, with a fresh scheme using his "Navajo" print in white impasto on a coarse emerald-green linen. The fabric was used for drapes and wall-coverings, and for the bed pelmet and canopy, which was fixed to the ceiling to create the impression of a four-poster bed. ABOVE: Commissioned to undertake the decoration of Alan Vetere's apartment in New York in 1971, David Hicks painted the concrete beams in the bedroom terracotta and used them to delineate the space. By covering the walls and ceiling in his "Arabic" wallpaper, Hicks also blurred the room's boundaries. Into this extravagant mix he introduced a "Celtic" rug on the parquet floor, a fur bedspread, burnt orange vinyl Roman shades, a lacquered table, and a mirror frame covered in one of his hexagonal prints.

ABOVE: A Paris bedroom by Maison Jansen, the Parisian design house established in 1880 by Jean-Henri Jansen (1854–1928), and under the creative direction of Stéphane Boudin (1888–1967) from the 1920s onward. The firm was known for mixing traditional European historical forms with new trends such as the Arts and Crafts movement, Turkish style, and Art Deco. OPPOSITE: The alcove in this grand bedroom at Nostell Priory in Yorkshire is furnished by designer David Mlinaric with an ornately draped four-poster bed. P120: One of 11 bedrooms in an 18th-century villa in the Tuscan town of Cetona, Italy. Realized by Lorenzo Mongiardino (1916–1998), the interior displays his characteristic sense of theater and use of artifice to create atmospheric spaces. P121: Detail of a bedroom by Mongiardino, who was revered for his ability to evoke lush romanticism in domestic interiors.

P122: The Paris bedroom of socialite Dodie Rosekrans, decorated by Tony Duquette (1914–1999), who had made his name in
Hollywood as a costume and set designer before attracting private
clientele for interior and jewelry commissions. P123: The master
bedroom in designer Tony Duquette's own home in San Francisco.
ABOVE: The Winter Bedroom at the Dawnridge Estate, Beverly Hills,

where Duquette lived with his wife Elizabeth from 1949. The interior was originally designed by Tony Duquette and adapted later by
Duquette's business partner Hutton Wilkinson. OPPOSITE: A guest
bedroom designed by Tony Duquette at the Palazzo Brandolini in
Venice, one of the palatial homes owned by Dodie Rosekrans.

ABOVE & OPPOSITE: French sculptor and designer Claude Lalanne (1924–2019) created her fanciful "Lit Singerie," or monkey bed, in 1999. Wrought from gilded bronze and copper, the bed is a frame of twisted vines and gingko leaves, from which four playful monkeys swing. Lalanne's client had wanted her bedroom to feel like a garden, and this was the artist's response. Inspired by Surrealism and Art Nouveau, Claude Lalanne often incorporated motifs from flora and fauna into her furniture. She worked with Yves Saint Laurent in the 1960s and 1970s, and from the 1980s onward with interior designer Peter Marino. **P128:** A French Empire bed is set against leopard-print wallpaper in the butterfly-themed bedroom in the former Turin home of architect, inventor and designer Carlo Mollino. Framed painted butterflies line the walls inside the canopied bed alcove. The house, Casa Mollino, is now a museum, its exquisite interiors kept intact since Mollino's death.

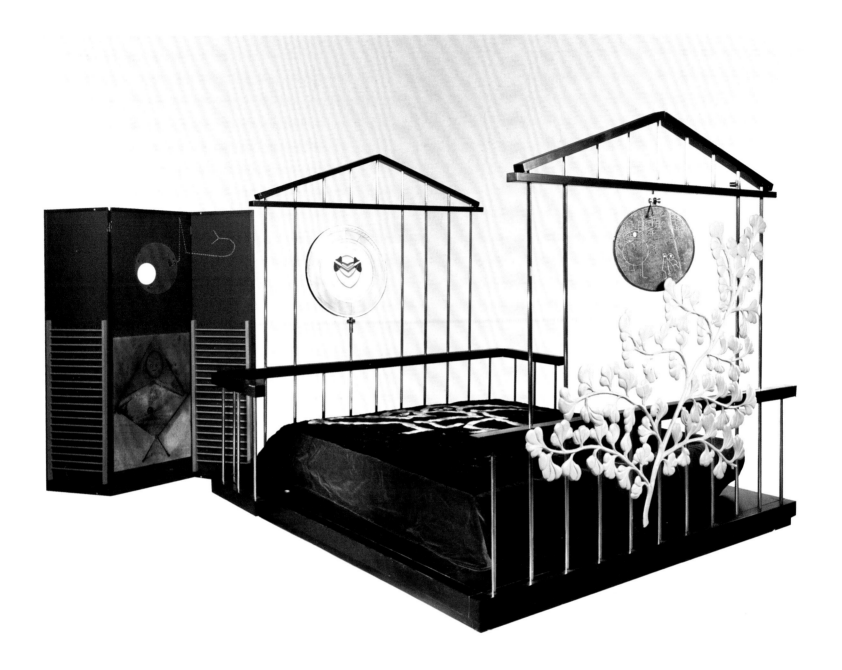

ABOVE: Dada pioneer and surrealist artist Max Ernst (1891–1976) designed this cage bed with screen in 1974. Made from African walnut, the headboard features the seal of Vice President of the United States—the bed was bought by Nelson Rockefeller, who served as vice president to Gerald Ford from 1974 to 1977. Rockefeller installed it in his official residence at Number One Observatory Circle, though he used the property mostly for entertaining. After he left office, Rockefeller offered the bed permanently to the house but it was turned down by subsequent vice presidents George W. Bush and Dan Quayle. **BELOW:** Curved, quilted walls and porthole windows feature in this bedroom in the Frey House in Palm Springs, which was designed by Albert Frey as his own residence. The circular master bedroom was added as a second story when the house was remodeled in 1953–54.

ABOVE: One of ten spherical bedroom suites in *Le Palais Bulles*, or Bubble Palace, designed by Hungarian-born architect Antti Lovag. The mural of planet-like orbs on the walls and ceiling is by Patrice Breteau. Built between 1975 and 1989 in Théoule-sur-Mer on the French Riviera, the house was conceived as a network of interconnecting bubble-like rooms. It expressed Lovag's idea that architecture should be joyful, playful, and spontaneous. Lovag rejected the interior tradition of classical lines, furnishing the bedrooms with circular beds and chairs. **OPPOSITE, ABOVE:** A painting by Jerome Tisserand adorns the rounded ceiling of a room in *Le Palais Bulles*. Each of the bedrooms was decorated by a different artist. **OPPOSITE, BELOW:** Guest rooms at *Le Palais Bulles*, which was originally built for French industrialist Pierre Bernard, and bought by Pierre Cardin in 1991.

OPPOSITE, ABOVE: Gio Ponti (1891–1979) and Piero Fornasetti (1913–1988) collaborated on this bedroom prototype for the Ninth Milan Triennale in 1951. The pair continued to work together for several decades, realizing a synthesis of ancient and modern. OPPOSITE, BELOW LEFT: As photographed by Horst for *Vogue* magazine in February 1970, an Op-art bedroom in the Paris apartment of French interior designer François Catroux and his wife Betty, then a model and muse to Yves Saint Laurent. OPPOSITE, BELOW RIGHT:

Cabriolet bed created in 1969 by Italian designer Joe Colombo (1930–1971), displayed in the Grassi Museum in Leipzig. The bed features a retractable canopy with a lighting system that simulates day or night, a built-in cigarette lighter, radio, telephone, and fan. ABOVE: The bedroom of Virginia Cowles in the apartment of her parents, publisher Gardner Cowles Jr. and philanthropist Jan Cowles. A Roy Lichtenstein print entitled "Brushstroke" hangs on the wall. The apartment was photographed by Horst for *Vogue* in 1971.

OPPOSITE & ABOVE: "Dream Beds" by Archizoom Associati from their intentionally kitsch Imperial Pink series of 1967. **P136:** A platform bed surrounded by four columns, created by Alessandro Mendini (1931–2019) in 1989. The columns are made from wood, serigraph-printed and lacquered, each with six glass shelves inside, and a blue crystal sculpture on top. Behind the bed is Gio Ponti and Paolo De Poli's enameled copper composition *Calle* (Calla Lilies) from 1940. At the base of the bed is *The Hope Chest* by Rhonda Zwillinger from 1986. The triptych on the left wall is part of the work. The painting on the ceiling is by Marco Rossati, 1990. **P137:** A series of four beds designed by Ettore Sottsass (1917–2007), entitled, from top left: *Mysterious*; top right, *The Societies on this Planet*; below left, *Unknown Vegetations*; below right, *At the Moment*. All were made in 1992.

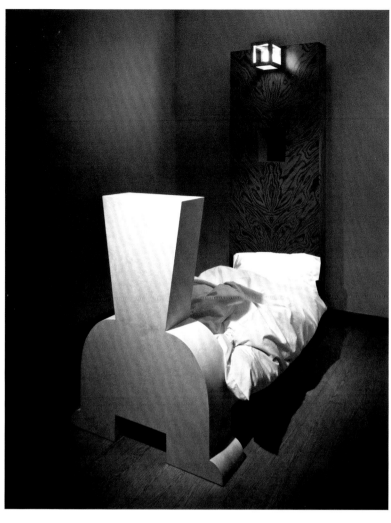

ABOVE: Swiss-born artist and furniture designer Mattia Bonetti was commissioned to decorate a Hong Kong apartment, which included this guest bedroom in shades of tangerine, with a one-off bed made by Bonetti. The bed sits on an orange lacquer platform, while a swathe of orange lacquer behind the bed sweeps up over the ceiling, serving as a virtual canopy. The headboard is padded with the same gray leather used for the bed covering. OPPOSITE: For the bedroom of the apartment owner's granddaughter, Mattia Bonetti created a bespoke scheme in teal and orange, with hand-painted wallpaper, a whimsical headboard and matching bedspread with orange and gold circular accents. He also designed the cast-bronze table lamp.

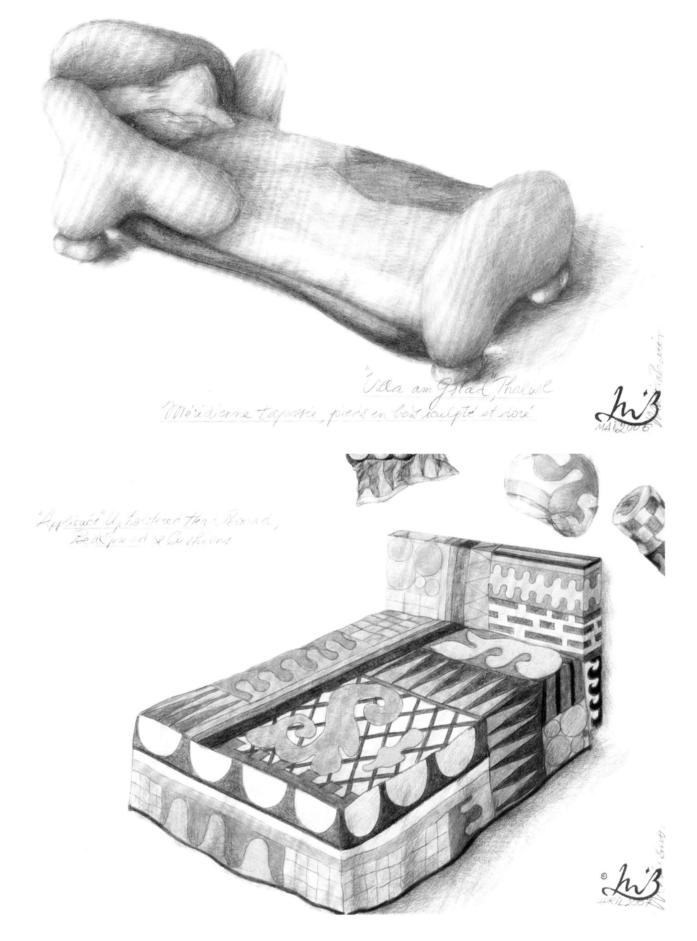

"Villa am Gstad" Thalwil
Méridienne tapissée, pieds en bois sculpté et doré
MAI 2006

"Appliqués" Upholstered Head Board,
Bed Spread & Cushions

ABOVE & OPPOSITE: Watercolor drawings for private commissions by Paris-based designer Mattia Bonetti, who is known in the art world for his inventiveness and love of striking color combinations. Bonetti studied textiles before becoming an interior designer in the 1970s, developing a sophisticated and imaginative neo-baroque style. His early commissions included devising the interior for Christian Lacroix's couture house in 1987, and the redesign of Picasso's Château de Boisgeloup in Paris. Elements of nature often infuse his work, evident in the "fire" and "water" beds [right, above and below]. His approach is always adventurous, expressing his belief that design "is about dreaming."

Star Chambers

Actors, Artists, Socialites & Writers

Andy Warhol once claimed that everything was more glamorous when done in bed—even peeling potatoes. Gandhi may have begged to differ, as he contemplated Indian politics from his spartan cot, although John and Yoko managed both glamor and gravitas when they staged a "bed-in" to promote world peace in 1969. W.C. Fields (who appeared on the cover of The Beatles *Sgt. Pepper* album) seemingly enjoyed his bed for only one purpose, declaring that sleep was the most beautiful experience in life—except drink. His onscreen cohort Mae West was quite the opposite, shunning drink and using her bed for a lot more than sleep – with mirrors on the ceiling of her all-white bedroom so she could see "how I'm doin'." Challenging West's reign as the ultimate sex symbol, a naked Marilyn Monroe seduced magazine readers from under the sheets, as did Ava Gardner, while Jayne Mansfield posed with her Pekingese in a powder pink bedroom that also featured in a controversial Playboy spread. Meanwhile, Lauren Bacall smouldered, fully clothed, on top of a neatly made double divan.

In bed, the creative mind incubates brilliant works of art, literature, and performance; beautiful men and women are seduced, and powerful people seek relief in more ways than one. Thus the bed has often provided subject matter for artists, a chance to explore deep-seated psychoses, and find liberation. Eugène Delacroix painted beds with passion and a degenerate eye, a clue to his self-confessed sexual frustration. Salvador and Gala Dalí had twin beds just far enough apart to keep their tempestuous relationship simmering, and Robert Rauschenberg and Tracy Emin made their own beds into artworks. Inside her monumental sculpture "Empress," Niki de Saint Phalle created a bedroom out of Venetian mirror fragments, and slept it in for several years. Artist Frida Kahlo had a particular attachment to her bed: confined to it for years after injuries sustained in a traffic accident, she painted many of her most iconic works here.

Like Frida, the flamboyant figures of the art, design, and film world have made their beds an extension of themselves. Rudolf Nureyev's Paris bedroom resembled a theatrical set, and Franco Zeffirelli slept in a tented fantasy in his Positano villa. Helena Rubinstein endeavored to get the beauty sleep she recommended to her customers, and ensured she looked her best while doing so in a Lucite bed designed by Ladislas Medgyes, with illuminated headboard and footboard to cast a flattering glow. Rubinstein was often dressed by Paul Poiret, who was photographed several times with his wife Denise in their bohemian bedroom. Another fashion legend, Diane von Furstenburg, lounged on leopard print for the camera lens, as did Twiggy at Biba, recreating the glamor of old Hollywood.

On the silver screen, the bedroom became a feat of art direction, notably the all-white bedroom in *One Heavenly Night* (1932), designed by Oliver Messel. It set the bar for films that followed, including *Dinner at Eight* (1933), in which Jean Harlow spends most of her time in bed. Hobe Erwin and Fredric Hope apparently used 11 shades of white for their designs, not including Jean Harlow's platinum hair, white satin negligees, and the white telephone on which she schemes how to climb the social ladder. Later, in color films, from *Cat on a Hot Tin Roof* to *A Space Odyssey*, the bed continued to play a starring role as a shrine to sexuality, and, as in real life, the backdrop for intimate fantasies and fears to be explored.

P143: Spanish artist Salvador Dalí lounges in his bedroom. P144, ABOVE LEFT: Gala and Dalí's bedroom at the Salvador Dalí House Museum in Port Lligat, Cadaques, Spain. P144, BELOW LEFT: "Venus Dreaming" from the series by Salvador Dalí, conceived for his "Dream of Venus" Pavilion at the World Fair in New York, 1939. Dali was forced to modify his original concept to make it more conservative for general public viewing. Nevertheless the pavilion succeeded in introducing Dalí's work, and the concept of Surrealism, to

a mass audience. P145: A surrealist bedroom at the Dalí Museum, Figueres, Spain. OPPOSITE: Jean Cocteau's (1889–1963) bedroom in his former home in Milly-la-Forêt, near Paris, decorated in collaboration with Madeleine Castaing. The bed was angled so that Cocteau could view the garden. ABOVE: Against a backdrop of his own illustrations on the bedroom wall, Jean Cocteau poses in 1957 during the shooting of the television programme "Live From," which was dedicated to the artist.

ABOVE: A 1937 self-portrait by Cecil Beaton (1904–1980), entitled
"Sunday Morning!" BELOW, LEFT: Beaton in his Circus Bed, as
shown in *Vanity Fair* magazine in 1934. BELOW, RIGHT: At his parents'
London home, Beaton papered the walls in floral damask adorned
with sequins and photographic cut-outs. OPPOSITE: Painted in 1939
by Sir Francis Cyril Rose (1909–1979), a watercolor of the Circus
Room, Beaton's bedroom at Ashcombe House, Wiltshire, England,
where he lived from 1930 to 1945.

The Circus Room at
Ashcombe.

Francis Rose 1939

P150/151: The Circus Bed was designed by Rex Whistler in 1931 and built by a specialist maker of carousels, Savages. The rococo-style bed incorporated the figures of Neptune and Cupid, underwater plants, unicorns, sea horses, and shells, and was draped in red and gold silk. The initials CB were wrought into the footboard. The recreation shown here was mounted for the "Cecil Beaton At Home" exhibition at Salisbury Museum in 2014. On the adjacent wall is a reproduction of the murals in the room painted by Cecil Beaton, Rex Whistler, and Oliver Messel. **ABOVE:** Horst P. Horst's bedroom at the home he built in 1949 at Oyster Bay, Long Island, part of the estate once owned by Louis Comfort Tiffany. **OPPOSITE:** Photographers Oberto Gili and Joy Sohn created a sense of bohemian glamor for the master bedroom of their farmhouse in Bra, Piedmont, Italy. The flower paintings are by Alida Morgan.

LEFT: Myrna Loy (as Fah Lo See) comforts Charles Starrett (as Terry Granville), after he is beaten at the hands of her father, on the bedroom set designed by Cedric Gibbons for *The Mask of Fu Manchu* (1932). Irish-born Gibbons, art director for MGM studios, was known for his innovative and sumptuous sets. **ABOVE**: One of a series of "bedroom" dramas directed by Cecil B. DeMille in the 1920s, *The Affairs of Anatol* (1921) cast Gloria Swanson as the stylish newlywed whose husband fools around until she, too, is tempted to have an affair. The art director was illustrator Paul Iribe, whose sets merged Art Nouveau and Art Deco styles. **BELOW**: Set Designers Richard Day and Joseph C. Wright created an abstract Moorish bedroom in *Blood and Sand* (1941) for the scene in which Doña Sol (Rita Hayworth) lies in waiting for a secret tryst with celebrity bullfighter Juan Gallardo (Tyrone Power).

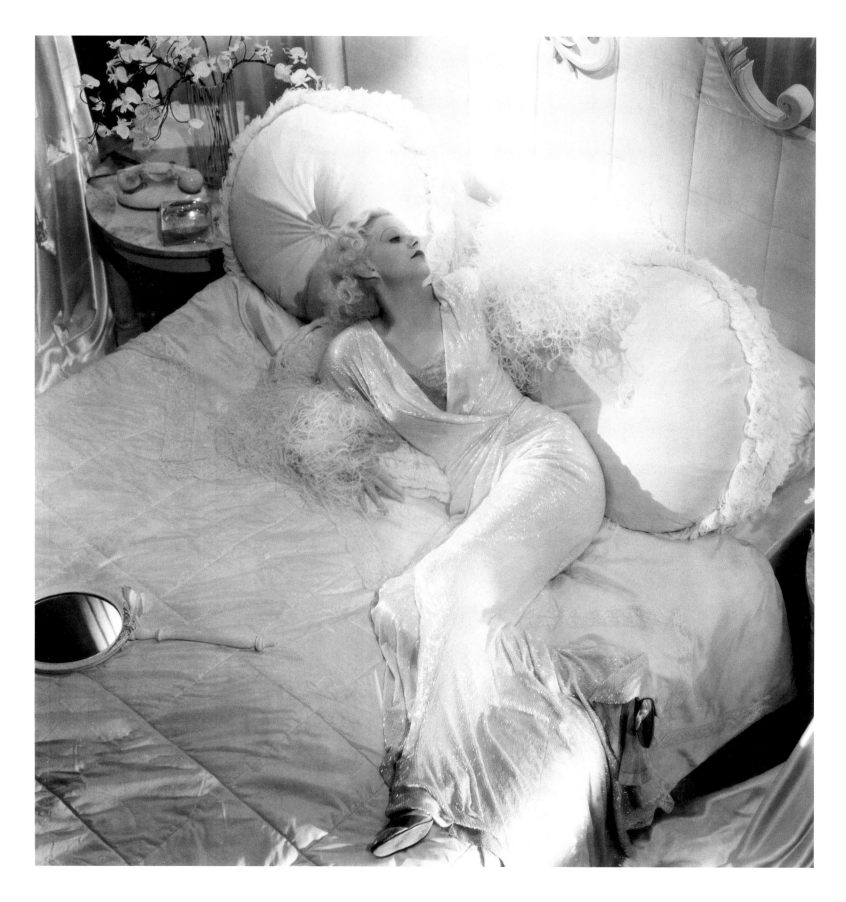

ABOVE: Playing the role of newly wealthy socialite Kitty, Jean Harlow lounges in bed planning an extravagant dinner party in a still from George Cukor's *Dinner at Eight* (1933). Art directors Hobe Erwin and Fredric Hope created an all-white Art Deco backdrop, and Adrian costumed Harlow in clinging white satin, to catch the light. One challenge emerged during the shoot: under the spotlights, the shadow of Harlow's dark pubic hair was visible through her gowns, requiring it to be bleached. OPPOSITE: The year before *Dinner at* *Eight*'s all-white film set, Oliver Messel conceived an entirely white bedroom for the C.B. Cochran-Max Reinhardt production of the Offenbach operetta *Helen!* at the Adelphi Theatre, London, in 1932. The lack of color on stage was considered revolutionary at the time; the approach in theater design was to always avoid an all-white set because it would flare under the lights and wash out the actors. Messel broke this cardinal rule but skillfully used shades of off-white and textured fabrics to avoid these issues.

LEFT: English stage actress Evelyn Laye made her Hollywood screen debut in *One Heavenly Night*, in 1931. The operetta was produced by Samuel Goldwyn, with Richard Day as art director. **ABOVE:** Mae West lolls in a gilded swan bed for the Broadway play *Diamond Lil* (1928), which she wrote and starred in. West purchased the bed from tycoon James Buchanan Brady, who had acquired it from the estate of the actress Amelia Bingham. The bed caught the imagination of *Time* magazine's theater critic, who wrote of Mae's character: "Diamond Lil was a harlot whose heart was as big and golden as the enormous swan-shaped bed that stood in her elaborate cubicle …" A different version of the swan bed later appeared in the play's film version *She Done Him Wrong* (1933). **BELOW:** A model reclines on a bed made of ostrich feathers during a private showing in 1934 of props from the film *Fashions of 1934*, directed by William Dieterie.

OPPOSITE, ABOVE: Against the Victorian Gothic set design of Charles D. Hall, actress Mae Clarke as newlywed Elizabeth languishes after an encounter with the monster (Boris Karloff) in *Frankenstein* (1931). OPPOSITE, BELOW: Douglas Fairbanks playing the title rolw of *The Thief of Bagdad* (1924) approaches the sleeping princess, while a maidservant, played by Anna May Wong, looks on. The Orientalist set design was by William Cameron Menzies. ABOVE: Erté's butterfly created an etheral mood for the bedroom set of *Sally, Irene and Mary* (1925). P162: Ginger Rogers on the set of *Shall We Dance?* (1937), designed by art director Van Nest Polglase. P163, ABOVE: Art director John DuCasse Schulze created the scheme for the romantic comedy *Twin Beds* (1942). P163, BELOW LEFT: Cedric Gibbons and Fredric Hope devised the Oscar-winning scenography for *The Merry Widow* (1934). Director Ernst Lubitsch is seen here in conversation with star Jeanette MacDonald. P163, BELOW RIGHT: Jeanette MacDonald in another scene from *The Merry Widow*.

P164, ABOVE LEFT: A silent film still captures the grandeur of Art Deco sets in the black and white era, when fluted design details, pleats, and folds were used to create shadows, lending a three-dimensional aspect to monochromatic interiors. P164, BELOW LEFT: Stephen Tennant photographed by Cecil Beaton. The youngest son of the 1st Baron Glenconner, Tennant was an eccentric English dandy who chose to spend the 17 last years of his life in bed. P165: English poet Edith Sitwell is served breakfast in bed, as shown in the pages of *Vogue* magazine,1932. OPPOSITE: In *Fall of the Roman Empire* (1964), set designers Veniero Colasanti and John Moore created a glamorized historical backdrop on an operatic scale. They also created the costumes worn by Sophia Loren (shown here) and the rest of the cast, including Alec Guiness, James Mason, Christopher Plummer, and Omar Sharif. ABOVE: Austrian actress Marisa Mell on a gilded swan bed in *French Dressing* (1964), directed by Ken Russell, with set decoration by Jack Stephens.

OPPOSITE, ABOVE LEFT: The quilted headboard was a recurring feature of Hollywood sets. Here, Italian actress Silvana Mangano smolders in a 1951 publicity still. OPPOSITE, ABOVE RIGHT: The bedside telephone call often provided narrative revelation and turning points: Bette Davis conducts morning business over breakfast in bed in *Mr. Skeffington* (1944), with art direction by Robert Haas. OPPOSITE, BELOW LEFT: Gloria Swanson, as the aging star Norma Desmond in *Sunset Boulevard* (1950), plays out a melodramatic scene on her frilly bed, while the object of her affections, played by William Holden, looks on. Set designers Sam Comer and Ray Moyer were joint Oscar winners for the film. OPPOSITE, BELOW RIGHT: A scene from *That Hamilton Woman* (1941), starring Vivien Leigh as Emma, Lady Hamilton. The film's director Alexander Korda employed Lyle R. Wheeler as art director to create the lavish backdrops. ABOVE: Art directors Roland Anderson and Hal Pereira set Carroll Baker on a round bed in a scene from *Harlow* (1965).

ABOVE: Rex Harrison as millionaire Cecil Fox in the ornate bedroom of his Venetian palazzo in a scene from *The Honey Pot* (1967). Production designer John DeCuir, art director Boris Juraga, and set decorator Paul S. Fox were responsible for the lavish look of the comedy drama. **OPPOSITE, ABOVE:** Writer Truman Capote rests in his hotel room in Holcomb, Kansas, during the filming of the movie *In Cold Blood* (1967), based on his novel. **OPPOSITE, BELOW LEFT:** Composer and writer Paul Bowles, pen and paper in hand, at home in Tangier around 1950. **OPPOSITE, BELOW RIGHT:** *Playboy* magazine publisher Hugh Hefner and his girlfriend, actress Barbi Benton, arrive aboard the customized Playboy DC-9 jet, "Big Bunny," in 1970. The plane's bedroom was kitted out with a circular waterbed, made up with silk sheets and Tasmanian possum-fur bedspread.

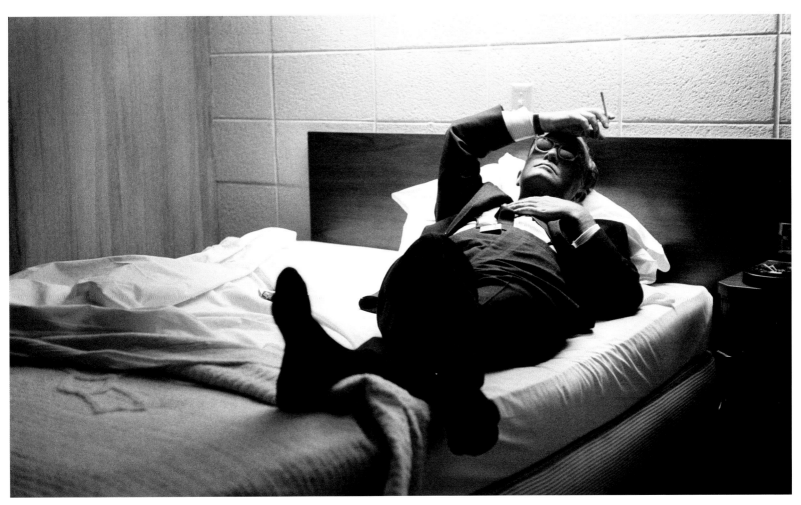

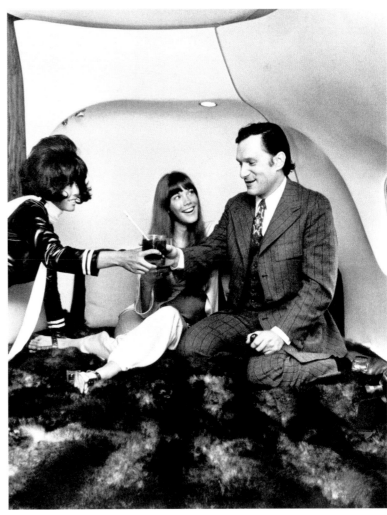

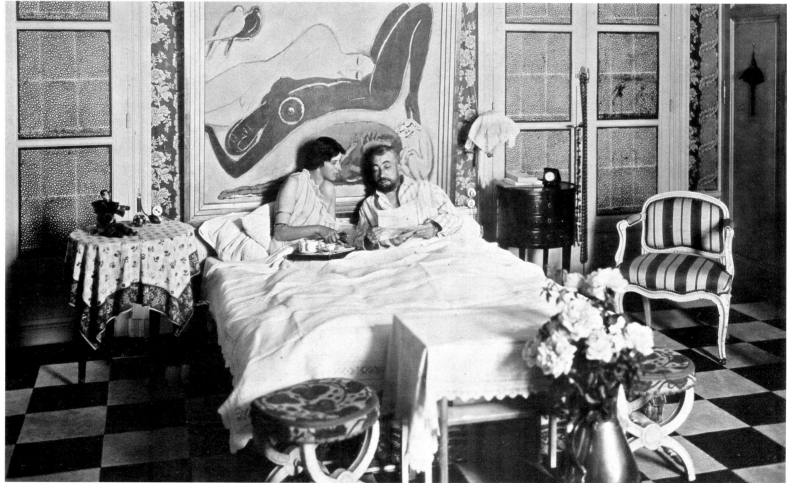

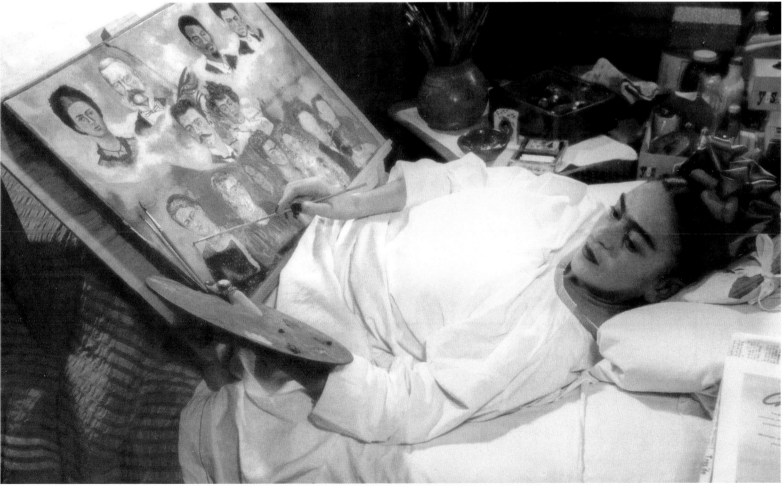

P172, ABOVE: Cosmetics tycoon Helena Rubinstein on her illuminated Lucite bed at home in New York in 1941, The bed was designed by Ladislas Medgyes and produced by Rohm & Haas in the late 1930s. P172, BELOW: Denise and Paul Poiret in their bedroom, photographed in 1932. P173, ABOVE: Ernest Hemingway at his typewriter ahead of his trip to Sweden to accept the Nobel Prize for Literature in 1954. P173, BELOW: Frida Kahlo painting in bed at home in Mexico City in 1952. OPPOSITE: American art collector, Peggy Guggenheim with an Alexander Calder sculpture behind her bed, photographed in 1961. ABOVE: Stars and comets decorate the wrought iron bed of Gabrielle "Coco" Chanel, photographed at her home, Villa La Pausa, in 1938.

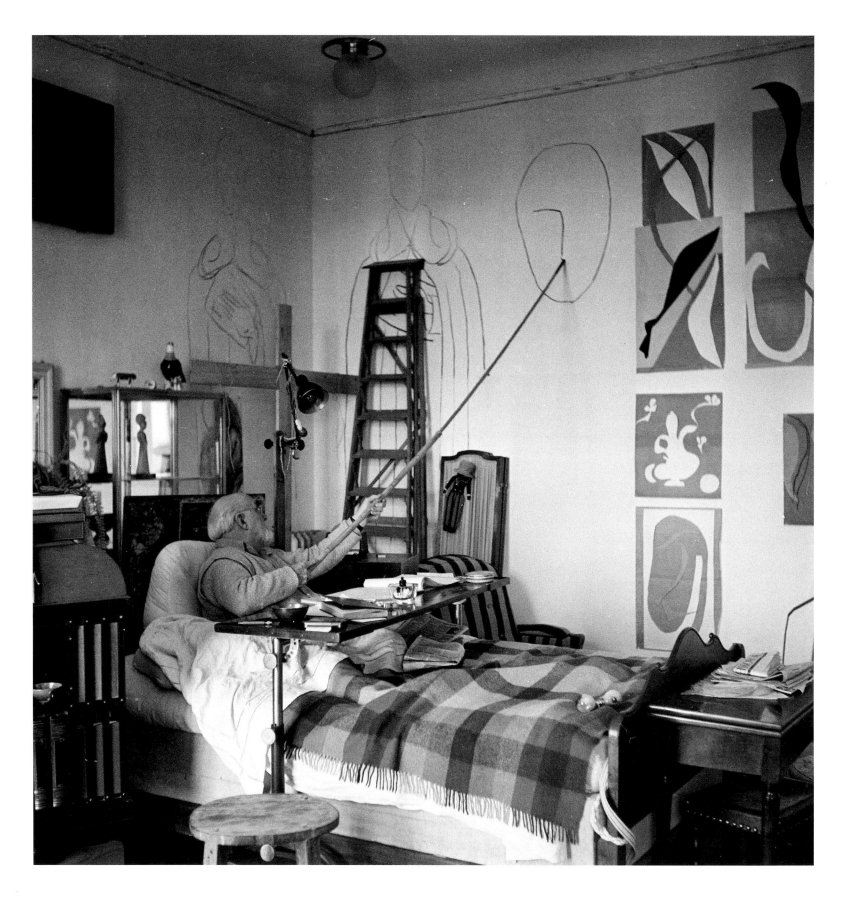

P176: Marilyn Monroe photographed by Cecil Beaton in a room at The Ambassador Hotel, New York, in February 1956. **P177, ABOVE:** American actress, Jayne Mansfield pictured on the set of *Too Hot to Handle* (1960), with bedroom set devised by art director Alan Withy. **P176, CENTRE:** Ava Gardner in satin sheets in 1945, the same year she married Lana Turner's ex-husband, Artie Shaw. **P176, BELOW:** Actress Lauren Bacall shows how to lounge with style, c. 1950. **ABOVE:** Artist Henri Matisse (1869–1954) in his apartment at the Palais Regina. Confined to bed after suffering a stroke, the artist used a piece of charcoal fixed to a stick to make his preparatory drawings for the frescoes of the Chapelle du Rosaire in Vence. **OPPOSITE:** Orson Welles directing the opening scene of the film *The Trial* (1962), based on the novel by Franz Kafka. The set was built at the abandoned Gare d'Orsay railway station in Paris under the art direction of Jean Mandaroux.

ABOVE: Art director Robert Usher realized a glamorous bedroom set in keeping with the style of nightclub owner Lady Lou, Mae West's seductive character in *She Done Him Wrong* (1933). **OPPOSITE:** Mae West at home in the penthouse of the Ravenswood apartment building in Hollywood Heights, where she lived from 1932. When residents complained about her then boyfriend, African-American boxer William Jones, and management barred him from entering the premises, West bought the entire building. Her rococo-style bed, with mirrors around and above it, was embossed with the letter "W." **P182:** Model Twiggy on a leopard-print bed at BIBA's Kensington store, 1971. **P183, ABOVE:** Actress Jayne Mansfield poses in 1960 in the bedroom of her Hollywood home, known as the Pink Palace, because of its pink interior scheme. **P183, BELOW:** Fashion designer Diane von Furstenberg at home in New York, 1978.

OPPOSITE: Elizabeth Taylor, photographed in a white negligee around 1950. ABOVE: Art director Lyle R. Wheeler won an Oscar for the period set designs in *Gone with the Wind* (1939), starring Clark Gable and Vivien Leigh. BELOW: Ann-Margret In *The Pleasure Seekers* (1964). P186, ABOVE: Bedroom in the home of fashion designer Jeanne Lanvin in rue Barbet-de-Jouy, Paris. The interior decoration is by architect Armand-Albert Rateau c. 1920–22, and the walls are covered with silk embroidered in the Lanvin workshops. The color is known as "Lanvin blue." P186, CENTER: Bedroom of Pyotr Ilyich Tchaikovsky. P186, BELOW: Jean Cocteau's bedroom at the Villa Santo Sospir, Cap Ferrat. P187: The Duchess of Windsor's bedroom in the villa she shared with the Duke of Windsor in Bois de Boulogne, Paris, decorated by Stéphane Boudin for Maison Jansen.

ABOVE: The State Bed designed by Édouard Lièvre (1828-1886) in 1875 for the French courtesan Émilie-Louise Delabigne, known as countess Valtesse de la Bigne, or by her nickname, "The Lioness." She was one of the most fashionable women in Paris, and her patrons ensured she lived in luxury: the Prince of Sagan have her a mansion on Boulevard Malesherbes, where the bed was much admired by friends privileged enough to be granted access. The

countess bequeathed the bed to the Musée des Arts Décoratifs.
OPPOSITE: The bedroom where notorious "womanizer" Giacomo Casanova stayed at the Morando Bolognini Castle, Sant'Angelo Lodigiano, Italy. The 18th-century bed is of the Piedmontese school, and is carved from soft wood, painted, and gilded. It is in stark contrast to the flea-infested pallet Casanova slept on in 1755 when imprisoned for "affront to religion and common decency."

P190: The bedroom of heiress and fashion designer Gloria Vanderbilt, as pictured in *Vogue* in 1970. The decor pays homage to American quilt heritage, with patchwork patterns covering the floor, walls, ceiling, and bed. **P191, ABOVE:** Solomon Guggenheim's Art Deco bedroom in his apartment at the Plaza Hotel in New York. **P191, BELOW:** William Randolph Hearst's bedroom at Hearst Castle in San Simeon, California. **ABOVE:** Pauline de Rothschild's chinoiserie-inspired bedroom in Paris, with 18th-century wallpaper and a tented taffeta bed with a faux bamboo metal frame. Pauline's apartment was on Rue Méchain in the 14th arrondissement, while her husband Philippe kept his own apartment in the 16th arrondissement. **OPPOSITE:** American socialite Dodie Rosekrans commissioned designer Tony Duquette and Hutton Wilkinson to create this dazzling blue and gold master bedroom in her home in Venice, the former Palazzo Brandolini, on the Grand Canal.

OPPOSITE: Rudolf Nureyev lived in New York's Dakota Building, on Central Park West, considered the city's first luxury apartment building. The interiors of the dancer's six-room apartment were said to be akin to stage sets, and his bedroom was no exception. Part of his collection of Old Masters can be seen on the walls. The bed itself is a carved oak and marquetry Elizabethan tester, covered with antique textiles. After Nureyev's death, his bed was sold at a Christie's auction in New York in 1995 for $255,500. **ABOVE:** One of the Moorish-style bedrooms in Rudolf Nureyev's former home on the island of Li Galli, near Positano, Italy. The island had been bought in 1922 by another famous dancer, Léonide Massine, who built a residence around the ruins of a 14th-century tower. After Massine's death, Nureyev purchased the island and became absorbed in redecorating the main villa.

ABOVE: The bedroom retreat of Oscar de la Renta, in the home he shared with his wife Françoise de Langlade at Casa de Campo in De la Renta's native Dominican Republic. The couple bought the compound, which they named Breeze House, in 1971. Designed by architect William Cox in the vernacular style, the four separate buildings were built from wood and decorated with cane furniture. This Horst photograph of the couple's bedroom appeared in *Vogue* magazine in 1974. OPPOSITE: Christian Louboutin's passion for Egyptian style is apparent in the bedroom of his adobe home, Dar El Baarat, near Luxor, Egypt. Against a tonal backdrop of terracotta-tiled floors and sand-colored walls, a few bold touches of local pattern are all that are needed to create a chic yet uncontrived atmosphere. It was only after purchasing the Luxor house that Louboutin discovered his biological father had been Egyptian.

ABOVE: American actress and dancer Ginger Rogers on the Art Deco-inspired mirrored daybed in her dressing room suite at the Theatre Royal, Drury Lane, London. The suite was decorated especially for her use during her 1969 appearance in the musical *Mame*. OPPOSITE, ABOVE: The white fur bed from the wardrobe room at Graceland, Memphis, the home of Elvis Presley. The photograph was taken for "The Tracks of the King" exhibition, held in May 2002, 25 years after his death. OPPOSITE, BELOW LEFT: Suspended daybeds on the porch of Doris Duke's home at her ShangriLa estate in Honolulu, as featured in *Vogue* magazine in 1966. OPPOSITE, BELOW RIGHT: Jewelry designer Paloma Picasso's study in her New York apartment, decorated with a French 19th-century swinging daybed. P200/201: A bedroom lined with shards of mirror in the *Giardino dei Tarocchi*, Garden of the Tarot, created by artist Niki de Saint Phalle (1930–2002) in Capalbio, Tuscany.

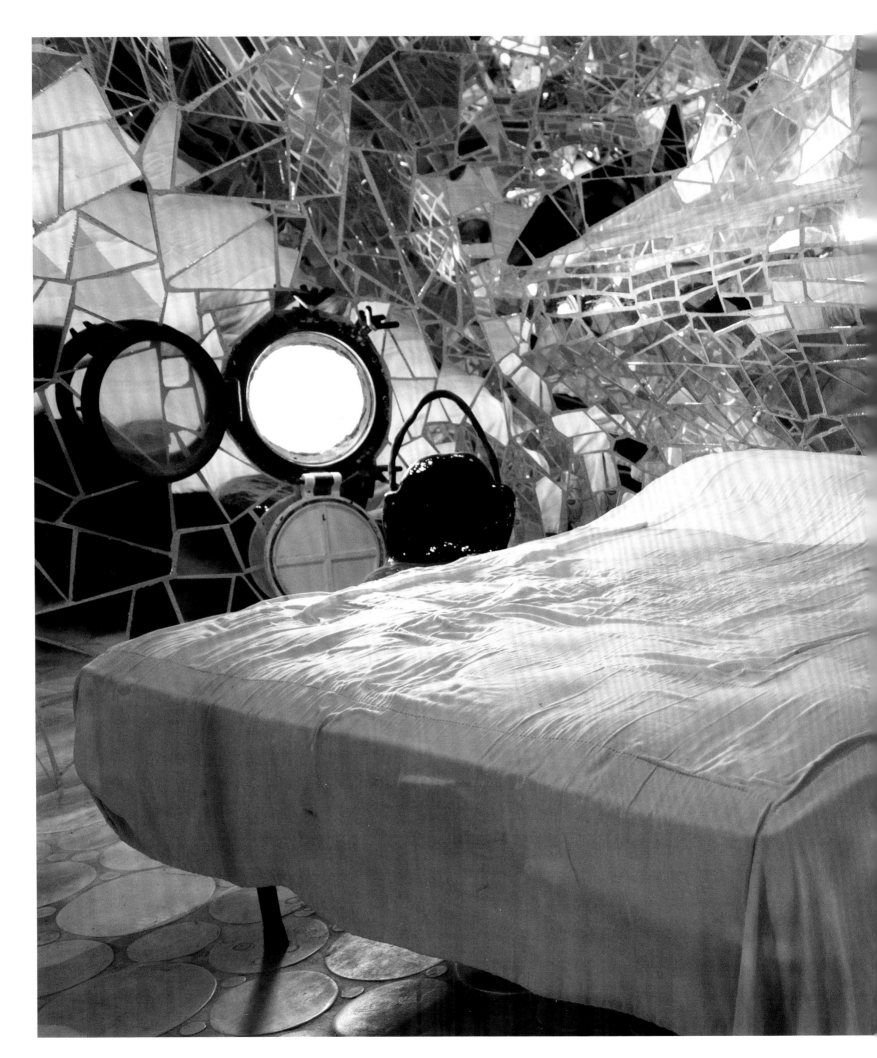

Contemporary Classics

From Hotel Living to Bijou Boudoirs

Literature's most famous insomniac, Marcel Proust, spent three years rarely able to sleep at night, and he was so desperate that he had his room in Paris lined in cork to block out noise. He might have taken heart from the knowledge that an estimated third of the French population now suffers from insomnia, much the same as in other major cities around the globe. Proust might also have marveled at the bedrooms of the 21st century, which at their best are devised to make slumber inevitable. The contemporary bedroom is not simply decorated; it is engineered—to deaden external sound, achieve the optimum lighting and temperature conditions, to create a place of refuge, isolated from the urban world.

Serenity reigns in Rick Owens' sparse bedroom for Salon 94, where a bed floats on a marble platform with a view to a leafy courtyard, and in Marco Bezzoli's Cape Town project, where an infinity pool extends from the end of the bed, overlooking the ocean. Other bedrooms look inward, blocking out the external world altogether. New York firm Snarkitecture transformed a tiny loft into a silent studio apartment lined with 25,000 ping pong balls. Andrée Putman, John Pawson, and Bunny Williams have curtained their beds to create intimate hideaways, while in fashion designer Lisa Perry's New York home a candy pink alcove is the setting for sweet dreams. The Enignum canopy bed by Joseph Walsh cradles the occupant in a sinuous wooden sculpture, and Eggarat Wongcharit's pod beds are like floating islands, swathed in netting hung from wicker canopies.

Some designers acknowledge that as well as being short on sleep, we may also find it hard to make time for seduction; Peter Marino, Francis Sultana, Carlos Mota, Studio Peregalli, and David Gill, for example, have all brought bohemian glamor and a sense of romance back to the bedroom. When we're not at home trying to catch up on sleep, and sex, we go on vacation to do so. And thus the art of cocooning has been honed by luxury resorts: Zaha Hadid's cave-like suite at the Hotel Puerta America; the pod-like villas of Bisate Lodge in Rwanda, set amidst pristine wilderness; or the princely decadence of the Taj Lake Palace hotel in Udaipur. Modern travelers are not the only ones to appreciate the appeal of a lifestyle that revolves around the bedroom. Coco Chanel lived at The Ritz, Paris; Margaret Thatcher at The Ritz, London, in the last years of her life. Peter Sellers lived at The Dorchester, where he met his second wife Britt Ekland. Richard Harris lived at The Savoy for 15 years. Cole Porter matched this, living the last 15 years of his life at the Waldorf Astoria. The hotel experience demonstrates that sometimes all you need is an ensuite bedroom—and room service. Or perhaps just a minibar. Designer Mathias Kiss opened the Kiss Room in 2013, a functioning art installation that served as a hotel room for 1000 nights in the Marais district of Paris. One thousand mirrors lined the 10-square meter room, reflecting its compact contents—a bed, a bathroom, and a refrigerator stocked with champagne.

P202: When fashion designer Lisa Perry bought her Upper East Side penthouse in 2000, she wanted to create the streamlined, futuristic mood of the 1960s, an era she had always been excited by. She and her husband commissioned 1100 Architect to carry out renovations, and engaged Tony Ingrao for the interior design. The mirror is by Ettore Sottsass. **OPPOSITE:** The scheme for this opulent bedroom by interior decorator Nicky Haslam is based on hangings in the staterooms of the city palace in Morbi, India. **ABOVE:** Nicky Haslam's initial model for the entrance hall at the 2011 Decorex International interior design show involved a silver shell bed, created by Wayne Clarke, in a romantic, if slightly surreal grotto bedroom. **BELOW:** A bedroom in Nicky Haslam's London apartment in the 1980s, with a mural by Paul Czainski.

P206/207: A guest bedroom in the château home of fashion designer Gérard Tremolet is dressed in Indian cashmere with the headboard upholstered in an antique carpet. **OPPOSITE:** This Venetian-inspired velvet bedhead with damask details was created by London-based interior designer Alidad. **ABOVE:** Twin beds under matching canopies in a guest bedroom at interior designer Jacques Garcia's 50-room Normandy château, Champ de Bataille. Garcia had visited the 17th-century castle as a boy of 12, and purchased it 34 years later when it was derelict, painstakingly restoring its original grandeur. **P210:** Interior designer John Stefanidis's bedroom at his home on Patmos reflects his eye for color and pattern. **P211:** Hand-painted walls by artist Lucas Risé in the style of enormous ceramic tiles subvert conventions of scale to create a playful mood in a bedroom in his Buenos Aires home.

P212: One of four simple bedrooms in the Tuscan home of interior designer Anthony Collett. Although the designer once shied away from using color, a passion for collecting pottery awakened an appreciation for bold hues, as is evident here in the handwoven textiles used for bedspreads and canopies. P213: A four-poster bed in the guest cottage of interior designer Muriel Brandolini's Hamptons home. **ABOVE:** An 18th-century Italian giltwood sunburst dominates this midnight-blue bedroom in the London home once shared by Hassan Abdullah, Michel Lasserre, and Stefan Karlson. **OPPOSITE:** Artist and sculptor Luigi Ontani created this wooden bed, entitled *Helioendimio*, in 1987. P216: The walls of a guest bedroom in this house in Milan, redecorated by Studio Peregalli, are covered in a 19th-century wallpaper. **P217, ABOVE:** In the French home of Ranuncho de St. Armand, a *lit à la Polonaise* is cluttered with objects, medallions, and paintings. **P217, BELOW:** Studio Peregalli decor using scenic wallpaper from the 19th-century.

P218: Parisian artist-designer Mathias Kiss reappropriates French classicism, preserving and updating historic codes by placing them in a contemporary context. P219: Green metallic fleur-de-lys wallpaper, blue and white tiles, an antique canopied bed, and gilt detailing strikes a mood of faded romance in the historic Dar Si Ahmed Tidjani at Aïn Mahdi, Algeria. OPPOSITE: Bright yellow walls reflect the Provençal sunshine in this house in St, Remy, home to French beauty entrepreneur Terry de Gunzburg. She honed her

sense of color while working for Yves Saint Laurent, and is known for her ability to combine unlikely shades to great effect. ABOVE: When interior designer Tino Zervudachi bought a house on the Greek island of Hydra in 2011, it was painted dark brown inside. Zervudachi transformed the interior with a palette of white, ecru, and dove gray. In the master bedroom, twill curtains by C&C Milano open to reveal the garden and view beyond. A Bhutanese textile serves as a bedspread.

ABOVE: "The Egyptian Wing" in the New York home of artist Izhar Patkin includes a sleeping chamber painted like an Egyptian tomb. Patkin collaborated on the interior design with Scooter LaForge, who painted the walls. Above the sarcophagus is a Hebrew inscription explaining that humans are not superior to animals. **BELOW:** Another painted retreat in Izhar Patkin's home. Dubbed "The Secret Garden Room," it was the first room in the house to be painted by LaForge. The floor lamp, made from bottles, was designed by Patkin. Kim MacConnel painted the bedspread and chair. **OPPOSITE:** The inspiration for the wall paintings in Patkin's "Grecian Guestroom" came from two sources: the room's original orange color scheme, and LaForge's love of ancient amphorae.

LEFT: The light-filled London home of chef Ruth and architect Richard Rogers was created from two derelict Georgian terraced houses, and decorated so that vibrant strokes of primary color pop against white walls and pale floors. In the master bedroom, a canary yellow bed with integrated shelving unit appears to float in a room devoid of clutter. The bed unit was commissioned from designer Ab Rogers, Richard's son, whose London studio fuses practicality and poetry to create entertaining yet functional furnishings and spaces.
ABOVE: A bright red wall enhances the sense of privacy in this low-key bedroom, created by architect Nicolas Vignot, which is separated from the living area by pivoting translucent panels.

OPPOSITE: A bedroom in the home of interior stylist Carlos Mota in the Dominican Republic. The room is carpeted in a woven floor-covering from Morocco, and the custom-made bed is covered with a Moroccan throw embellished with pompoms. A Picasso-inspired wall mural is another playful touch, as is the throw cushion embroidered with Mota's name. ABOVE: The master bedroom in the modernist villa shared by filmmaker Katrine Boorman and artist Danny Moynihan in Oualidia, Morocco. It features a Beni Ourain carpet and Berber fabrics, with a painting by Danny's father Rodrigo Moynihan. The room opens onto a courtyard filled with traveler's palms, jasmine vines, and rosebushes. P228/229: Owned by the writer Susana Bombal, Los Alamos nestles in the foothills of the Andes in Argentina. The painting on canvas that hangs behind the twin iron-framed beds in this guest bedroom was one of her spontaneous purchases.

OPPOSITE: A hand-embroidered suzani covers the wall of New York-based artist Holly Lueders' bedroom in the cottage she restored on the Greek island of Patmos with the help of designer Tetty Stefanou. Lueders has been visiting Greece since she was an 18-year-old student of art history and archaeology at Columbia University. She returned to Greece every year thereafter, completing her studies in Athens, and building a collection of traditional Greek clothing and textiles. The bed coverlet is made from fragments of 19th-century curtain fabric from the island of Kos, its faded colours echoed in the striped ceiling. ABOVE: The bedroom of antique dealer and collector the late Christopher Gibbs in his former apartment at Albany, in London's Piccaddilly. The mansion was designed for Viscount Melbourne in the 1770s. In keeping with Albany tradition, Gibbs was assessed by the building's trustees, and had to agree to adhere to the rules: "No pets, no children, no whistling, no noise, and absolutely no publicity."

ABOVE: Tickings and ikats from Robert Kime's antique textile collection cover a daybed on the top floor of the belvedere at Swangrove, the Duke of Beaufort's hunting lodge on the Badminton Estate, in Gloucestershire. OPPOSITE: Camilla Guinness's bedroom at her home in Tuscany, with murals painted by Virginia Loughnan. P234: Katharine and William Rayner commissioned architect Peter Marino to help renovate their 1930s cottage, Woody House, on Long Island's eastern tip. A master bedroom was added as a second story, commanding views over Georgica Pond and the Atlantic Ocean. Marino devised a patterned interior in faded reds, inspired by a cotton fabric the Rayners found in Mumbai. P235: Christopher Gibbs' former bedroom at Clifton Hampden in Oxfordshire is furnished with a ceramic four-poster bed with leaf-wrapped pillars. It was made in the 1830s by the Staffordshire ironstone china factory established by Miles Mason.

ABOVE: Alphonsine doors screened with antique silk curtains open to an 18th-century Olotina bed in the home of Spanish interior designers Chantal and Raimon Soler in the historic city of Empúries on the Mediterranean coast of Catalonia. When they bought the ancient manor house it was in a dilapidated state, but the couple brought it back to life with a restrained palette and antique furnishings spanning several centuries. The bedroom walls were layered with coats of lime wash to create an aged patina.

OPPOSITE: When Peter Marino was approached by Katharine and William Rayner to rethink their house in Palm Beach, he took the couple's love of exotic travel as his starting point, merging Ottoman and Moroccan crafts and architectural styles. Guest quarters were positioned at either end of the house to ensure privacy. This guest bedroom references the Topkapi Palace in Istanbul, with a domed ceiling, rich metallic details, and an opulent mix of Arab-inspired patterns and colors encasing the room.

OPPOSITE & ABOVE: American designer Bunny Williams reveals her penchant for comfort with these two different styles of four-poster bed. She often uses four-poster beds as they make a room look taller, and also create the effect of a room within a room. The trick is to scale any furniture to suit the size of the room; it shouldn'tt be too big, but an even worse mistake is to have furniture that is too small. When it comes to soft furnishings, Williams always piles beds high with pillows, and prefers beautiful throws and blankets to duvets. Williams worked for legendary American designer Sister Parish before starting out on her own in 1988.

ABOVE: This twin bedroom in interior designer Katy Barker's holiday home on the Kenyan island of Lamu has been finished with raw plaster and the bed hangings decorated with local embroidered textiles. OPPOSITE: A brightly colored Masai beaded chair in Emma Wilson's simple, whitewashed bedroom in Morocco. P242: The

London bedroom of Peter Hone celebrates his profession as a master of plaster casting. P243: This bedroom by interior designer Juan Montoya in the Dominican Republic features a custom-designed headboard inset with plaster forms and a chandelier by Stephen Antonson. The bed is dressed with Mexican textiles.

P244: A daybed occupies a corner of this bedroom at the Albergo Diffuso Le Grotte della Civita in southern Italy, a small hotel created in a series of restored caves. P245: In the Tangier home restored by Nadia and Suomi La Valle, an antique English canopied iron bed, made for the colonial market in the mid-19th century, is dressed with soft furnishings in stripes and more elaborate Arab-influenced prints and patterns. OPPOSITE: The bedroom of a boutique-style luxury lodge in Kenya takes the form of a treehouse constructed entirely of wood and rushes, with the talents of many local artists contributing to the finishing touches. ABOVE: The holiday home of Parisian antique dealer and collector Patrick Perrin in Comporta, Portugal, is furnished in shades of white and sand with copious amounts of vintage rattan, wicker, and rope furniture.

OPPOSITE: One of six luxurious forest villas at Bisate Lodge in Rwanda. The richly detailed interiors employ a variety of woven materials, drawing on Rwandan craft traditions. **ABOVE:** Created by Hudson Architects, the Feeringbury Barn Silo in Essex is a corrugated grain silo, which has been converted to provide additional guest accommodation comprising a bedroom and shower room. **P250:** San Francisco-based Ken Fulk designed this contemporary bedroom with a traditional British feel at Birch Castle in San Francisco's Pacific Heights. Fulk renovated the five-story home for the founders of tech entrepreneurs Michael and Xochi Birch, who developed the social networking platform Bebo. **P251:** A custom-made four-poster bed and antique antler chairs furnish the master bedroom decorated by Ken Fulk at the "Halfway House" lodge in the mountain resort of Big Sky, Montana. The designer cleverly used salvaged wood from snow fences and old barns for the interior walls and floors.

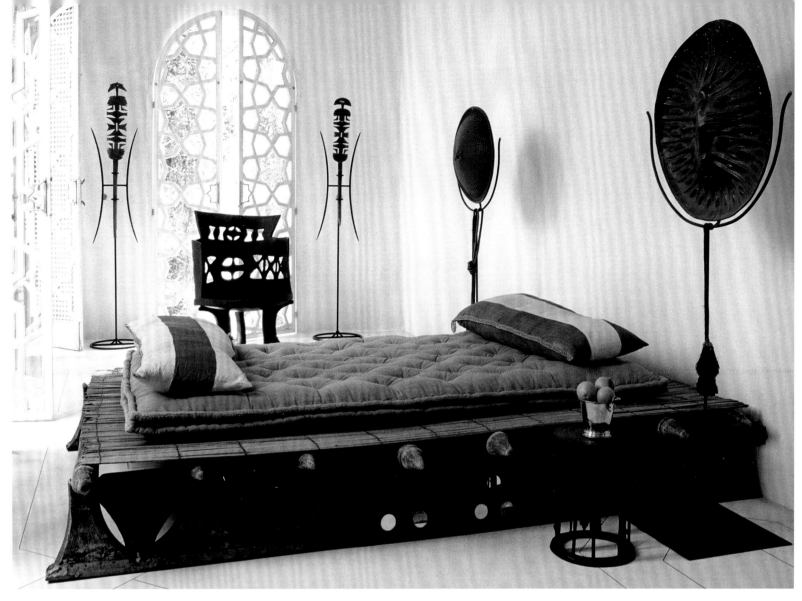

P252: The Chandra Prakash Suite, or Luster of the Moon Suite, at the Taj Lake Palace hotel in Udaipur. P253, ABOVE: Ethiopian shields stand sentinel either side of a carved African platform bed in this simply furnished guestroom at the Moroccan home of fashion designer Liza Bruce and her husband, artist Nicholas Alvis Vega. P253, BELOW: A wrought-iron four poster bed is decked with local rugs on a roof terrace at the Pantelleria home of architect Flavio Albanese. ABOVE: A four-poster bed in a Bedouin-style tented bedroom at Jack's Camp, Botswana. OPPOSITE: One of nine ensuite tents at Singita Sabora Tented Camp, Grumeti, Tanzania. Each one is decorated with antiques, artefacts, and original safari furniture, along with Zanzibari chests, Perisan rugs, local Masai blankets, and traditional beadwork. At night the tents are illuminated by brass hurricane lamps.

OPPOSITE: Jeanne Bayol creates a bohemian fantasy in the interior of her gypsy caravan, or roulotte, in St.-Rémy-de-Provence, set in a clearing of Cypress trees. ABOVE: Jewelry designer Carolyn Roumeguère's feminine bed sits beneath a cloud of mosquito netting in a stilted African mud hut. It is furnished with rugs and personal accessories collected during her adventures in Africa. This simply adorned bedroom reflects her nomadic upbringing—her stepfather was a Masai warrior and her mother a social anthropologist. P258: Mattresses the color of the sea have been fitted on a narrow roof terrace overlooking the Bay of Naples at the historic Miramare di Sant'Angelo hotel on the island of Ischia. Architect Giuliano Andrea dell'Uva was engaged to give the hotel a new look. P259: A hotel bedroom on the island of Milos, Greece.

OPPOSITE: The Razor House by architect Wallace Cunningham is designed to capture the beauty of the surrounding Torrey Pines State Natural Reserve near La Jolla in San Diego, California. Walls of white Portland cement, floor-to-ceiling glass panels, and large-scale open spaces give the house the feel of an art gallery. **ABOVE:** This modern American house, built by architect Will Meyer, is conceived as a series of boxes suspended from concrete beams and clad in sheets of glass. **P262:** Architect Marco Bezzoli designed this master bedroom, viewed across the outdoor swimming pool against the spectacular backdrop of Cape Town's Table Mountain. **P263:** Resin floors in green and silver underpin this bedroom scheme at the Miramare di Sant'Angelo hotel on the island of Ischia, with architecture and interiors by Giuliano Andrea dell'Uva. The 1950s glass chandelier was salvaged from a Miramare warehouse.

LEFT: Shades of green punctuate a serene guest bedroom at designer Francis Sultana's home in Malta. Sultana designed the console table and bed. The armchair is from specialist rattan furniture maker Bonacina 1889, and the curtains are from Loro Piana. The lithograph is by Francesco Clemente ("Semen," 1987). **ABOVE:** Gallerist David Gill designed the backlit bed in the master bedroom of his London home. He also made Francesco Clemente's '"Semen" a focal point for the room. **P266:** This bedroom in the Villa Siam at the Iniala Resort, Phuket, was designed by Eggarat Wongcharit, who employs traditional Thai skills, such as wicker weaving, in a 21st-century style. **P267, ABOVE:** Fashion designer Rick Owens channels the brutalist aesthetic of Le Corbusier's modernism for his furniture designs, while his use of rare materials, such as alabaster, alludes to the beauty of nature. **P267, BELOW:** Made of olive, ash, and organza, the *Enigmum I Canopy Bed*, the first in an edition of twelve by Joseph Walsh, is displayed at the National Museum of Ireland.

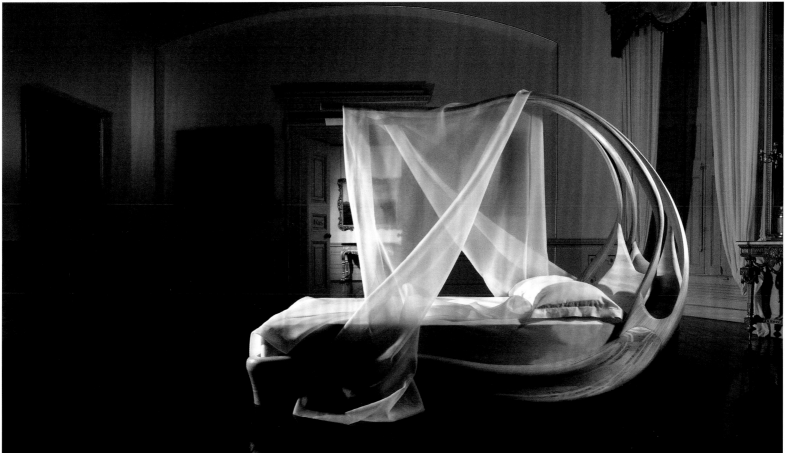

ABOVE: Bedroom at the Lecam Residence in the Hollywood Hills, conceived by architect Atelier VB, the Los Angeles studio of Vianney Boutry. Floor-to-ceiling glass walls maximize the outlook, which stretches from the Griffith Observatory to the Pacific Ocean. BELOW: As featured in *Vogue* magazine in 1972, a bedroom in the Japanese-style house designed by American architect Bruce Goff. OPPOSITE: The bed created by Italian architect and designer Gaetano Pesce for Marc-André Hubin resembles a giant paper-and-twine-wrapped package. "Think about a bed," he says. "If you go to bed with someone, you don't know what might happen. The bed represents that." A system of pulleys opens up the "package" to reveal the mattress inside. P270/271: Clean, mid-century lines define this bedroom in a contemporary home designed by Luis Laplace on the Spanish island of Ibiza. P272/273: Laplace also turned his hand to this vibrant Paris apartment, unifying the bedrooms with monochromatic wallpaper in patterns found in nature, combined with pop colors of apple green, orange, and bright purple.

ABOVE: An igloo-like room at the Hotel Puerta America in Madrid designed by Zaha Hadid Architects. The bed is integrated into the room's wall molding. **BELOW:** Designed by Petros Dermatas and Ellie Souti, Cesare's Wake Suite at the Icehotel, Jukkasjärvi in Sweden is furnished with a bed draped in reindeer skins. **OPPOSITE:** Designed by Matthias Kiss in 2013, The Kiss Room was an art installation and pop-up hotel room inside La Perle, a café in the Marais district of Paris. Measuring just 10 square meters, the mirror-lined room was open for 1,000 nights; guests could book for one night only. **P276/277:** The wall in antique dealer and decorator Florence Lopez's Paris studio is painted in homage to Brazilian landscape artist Roberto Burle Marx. A George Nakashima bed is teamed with a 1947 Arne Norell chair and Carlo Mollino lamp.

P278/279: A bedroom in a Hawaiian house designed by architect Tom Kundig and designer Rodman Primack. **OPPOSITE, ABOVE:** "The Barmecide Feast," a reproduction of the famous bedroom from Stanley Kubrick's *2001: A Space Odyssey*, on display at the National Air and Space Museum in Washington DC. **OPPOSITE, BELOW LEFT:** A low-ceilinged bedchamber in a house designed by Daniel Libeskind. **OPPOSITE, BELOW RIGHT:** Artwork for Pink Floyd's album cover *A Momentary Lapse of Reason*, released in 1987 and exhibited at the V&A, London, in 2017. **ABOVE:** Transparent, inflatable bubble tents in Guilin, Guangxi Zhuang Autonomous Region of China. The idea is to allow visitors to stay in touch with nature. **P282/283:** Daniel Arsham sculpts, paints, and runs his architecture firm, Snarkitecture, with Alex Mustonen, in Greenpoint, Brooklyn. When he decided to live above the studio, he converted a 90-square-metre loft into a bedroom studio lined with 25,000 ping pong balls.

Credits

Photography Credits

Best efforts were made to verify all photography and art credits. Any oversight was unintentional and should be brought to the publisher's attention so that it can be corrected in future printing.

P2: © James Fennell / The Interior Archive

P4: © George Rinhart / Corbis via Getty Images

P6: © Edmond Duthoit / Bridgeman Images

P8-9: Horst P. Horst / © Condé Nast via Getty Images

P10: © Adam Butler / The Interior Archive

P12: © Tim Clinch / Riviera Style

P13: © Werner Forman / Universal Images Group / Getty Images

P14: Giovanni Battista Castello (1509-1569), donated to the Victoria & Albert Museum by Dowager Viscountess Harcourt GBE / © Victoria & Albert Museum, London

P15 ABOVE: Paul Gardner, © Victoria & Albert Museum, London **BELOW:** Unidentified author / Alinari / Getty Images

P16: © Luca Tettoni / Bridgeman Images

P17: © Fritz von der Schulenburg / The Interior Archive

P18-19: © Harald Wenzel-Orf / Image Broker / Agefotostock

P20: © Francesco Venturi

P22/23: © Francesco Venturi

P24: © Victoria and Albert Museum, London

P25: © Christopher Simon Sykes / The Interior Archive

P26: © Alex Ramsay / The Interior Archive

P27: © Christopher Simon Sykes / The Interior Archive

P28: © Musée National du Chateau de Malmaison / Bridgeman Images

P29: © G Dagli Orti / De Agostini Picture Library / Getty Images

P30 ABOVE: © Gerhard Trumler / Imagno / www.picturedesk.com **BELOW:** © AKG-images / Erich Lessing

P31: © Christopher Simon Sykes / The Interior Archive

P32: © Fritz von der Schulenburg / The Interior Archive

P33: © Fritz von der Schulenburg / The Interior Archive

P34: © Simon Upton / The Interior Archive

P35: © Richard Bryant / Arcaid Images

P36: © G Cigolini / AKG-images / De Agostini Picture Library

P37: © Francesco Venturi

P38 ABOVE: © AKG-images / Heritage-Images / The Print Collector **BELOW LEFT:** © agefotostock Art Collection / Alamy Stock Photo **BELOW RIGHT:** © David Lefranc / Gamma-Rapho via Getty Images

P39: © Simon Upton / The Interior Archive

P40: © Mark Luscombe-Whyte / The Interior Archive

P41: © AKG-images / Jean-Claude Varga

P42-43: © Jacques Dirand / The Interior Archive

P44: © Antonio Monfreda, courtesy *Cabana* Magazine

P45: © Mark Luscombe-Whyte / The Interior Archive

P46 ABOVE: Franz Xavier Nachtmann / Bridgeman Images **BELOW:** © Jacques Dirand / The Interior Archive

P47: © Simon Upton / The Interior Archive

P48: © G Nimatallah / De Agostini Picture Library / Getty Images

P49: © Fritz von der Schulenburg / The Interior Archive

P50: AKG-images / Erich Lessing

P51: © A Dagli Orti / De Agostini Picture Library / Getty Images

P52: © Fritz von der Schulenburg / The Interior Archive

P53: © James Fennell / The Interior Archive

P54-55: © James Fennell / The Interior Archive

P56: © Miguel Flores-Vianna, courtesy *Cabana* Magazine

P57: © Christopher Simon Sykes / The Interior Archive

P58: © Anne Garde

P59: © Anne Garde

P60-61: © Anne Garde

P62: © Mark Luscombe-Whyte / The Interior Archive

P63: © Fernando Bengoechea / Getty Images

P64: © Antonio Monfreda, courtesy *Cabana* Magazine

P65: © AKG-images / Fratelli Alinari

P66: Education Images / UIG via Getty Images

P67: © Fernando Bengoechea / Corbis

P68-69: © Christopher Simon Sykes / The Interior Archive

P70: © Alexandre Bailhache / Claude Lalanne / DACS

P72: © Firooz Zahedi

P73: © Fritz von der Schulenburg / The Interior Archive

P74: © Fritz von der Schulenburg / The Interior Archive

P75: © travelibUK / Alamy Stock Photo

P76: Courtesy Kindel Furniture / © Dorothy Draper & Company Inc

P77: Peter Nyholm / © Condé Nast via Getty Images / Henri Matisse / DACS

P78 ABOVE: Buffotot / © Condé Nast via Getty Images **BELOW LEFT:** Architectural Press Archive / RIBA Collections **BELOW RIGHT:** Patrice Schmidt © CNAC / MNAM / Dist. RMN-Grand Palais / Art Resource, NY

P79: © Bonney / Ullstein Bild via Getty Images

P80 ABOVE & BELOW: © Galerie Patrick Seguin / Jean Prouvé / DACS

P81 ABOVE: © MAD, Paris / Photo Jean Tholance / Andre Arbus / Vadim Androusov

P149: Photograph by James McMillan © The Cecil Beaton Studio Archive at Sotheby's

P150-151: © James McMillan, courtesy Beaudesert Ltd

P152: © Fritz von der Schulenburg / The Interior Archive

P153: © Oberto Gili

P154: © Glasshouse Images / REX / Shutterstock

P155 ABOVE: © Paramount / Kobal / REX / Shutterstock **BELOW:** © 20th Century Fox / Kobal / Shutterstock

P156: © Bettmann via Getty Images

P157: © Sasha / Stringer via Getty Images

P158: © Bettmann via Getty Images

P159 ABOVE: © Kobal / Shutterstock **BELOW:** © Topical Press Agency / Getty Images

P160 ABOVE: © Universal / Kobal / Shutterstock **BELOW:** © Granger / Shutterstock

P161: © MGM / Kobal / Shutterstock

P162: © George Rinhart / Corbis via Getty Images

P163 ABOVE: © United Artists / Kobal / Shutterstock **BELOW:** ©AKG-images / Album / MGM

P164 ABOVE: © Granger / REX / Shutterstock **BELOW:** © The Cecil Beaton Studio Archive at Sotheby's

P165: Cecil Beaton / © Condé Nast via Getty Images

P166: © Granger / Shutterstock

P167: © Les Lee / *Daily Express* / Hulton Archive / Getty Images

P168 ABOVE LEFT: © Philippe Halsman / Magnum Photos

ABOVE RIGHT: © Warner Bros / Kobal / Shutterstock **BELOW LEFT:** © Paramount / Kobal / Shutterstock **BELOW RIGHT:** © Laszlo Willinger via John Kobal Foundation / Hulton Archive / Getty Images

P169: © Archive Photos / Stringer / Paramount Pictures / Getty Images

P170: © Michael Ochs Archives / Stringer / United Artists / Getty Images

P171 ABOVE: © Steve Schapiro / Corbis via Getty Images **BELOW LEFT:** © Jerry Cooke / Pix Inc / The *Life* Picture Collection via Getty Images **BELOW RIGHT:** © AFP Photo / Central Press / Stringer / Getty Images

P172 ABOVE: © Herbert Gehr / *Time* & *Life* Pictures via Getty Images **BELOW:** © Ullstein Bild via Getty Images

P173 ABOVE: © Tore Johnson / Magnum Photos **BELOW:** © Juan Guzman / Granger Historical Picture Archive / Alamy Stock Photo / Frida Kahlo / DACS

P174: © Ullstein Bild via Getty Images / Alexander Calder / DACS

P175: © Granger Historical Picture Archive

P176: © The Cecil Beaton Studio Archive at Sotheby's

P177 ABOVE: © Popperfoto via Getty Images **CENTRE:** MGM / Kobal / Shutterstock **BELOW:** © Silver Screen Collection via Getty Images

P178: © Walter Carone / *Paris Match* via Getty Images / Henri Matisse / DACS

P179: © Nicolas Tikhomiroff / Magnum Photos

P180: © Paramount / Kobal / REX / Shutterstock

P181: © Kobal / Shutterstock

P182: © Justin de Villeneuve / Hulton Archvie via Getty Images

P183 ABOVE: © Allan Grant / The *Life* Picture Collection via Getty Images **BELOW:** © Robert R McElroy / Getty Images

P184: © Hulton Archive via Getty Images

P185 ABOVE: © Silver Screen Collection / Archive Photos via Getty Images **BELOW:** Photo by Camerique / Getty Images

P186 ABOVE: © AKG-images / Erich Lessing **CENTRE:** © De Agostini Picture Library / Getty Images **BELOW:** AKG-images / Patricia Sigerist / Jean Cocteau / DACS

P187: © Fritz von der Schulenburg / The Interior Archive

P188: © Philippe Chancel / AKG-images / © Les Arts Décoratifs, Paris

P189: © G Cigolini / AKG-images / De Agostini Picture Library

P190: Horst P. Horst / © Condé Nast via Getty Images

P191 ABOVE: © A Dagli Orti / De Agostini Picture Library / Getty Images **BELOW:** Visions of America / UIG via Getty Images

P192: Horst P. Horst / © Condé Nast via Getty Images

P193: © Fernando Bengoechea

P194: © Fritz von der Schulenburg / The Interior Archive

P195: © Francesco Venturi

P196: Horst P. Horst / © Condé Nast via Getty Images

P197: © Deidi von Schaewen / Artedia / VIEW

P198: © Rolls Press / Popperfoto via Getty Images

P199 ABOVE: © David Lefranc / Gamma-Rapho via Getty Images **BELOW LEFT:** Horst P. Horst / © Condé Nast via Getty Images

BELOW RIGHT: Horst P. Horst / © Condé Nast via Getty Images

P200-201: © Olaf Kruger / ImageBroker / REX / Shutterstock / Niki de Saint Phalle / DACS

P202: © Peter Aaron / Otto / Ettore Sottsass / DACS

P204: James Mortimer / *The World of Interiors* © Condé Nast Publications Ltd

P205 ABOVE: Courtesy Quarto Books **BELOW:** © Fritz von der Schulenburg / The Interior Archive

P206-208: © Simon Upton / The Interior Archive

P209: © Mark Luscombe-Whyte / The Interior Archive

P210: © Fritz von der Schulenburg / The Interior Archive

P211: © Matthieu Salvaing

P212: © Simon Upton / The Interior Archive